MY HAUNTED COLLECTION

By

Kevin Cain

Other Books by Kevin Cain

FICTION

Patty Doll

Haunts

NON-FICTION

The Legends of Indian Narrows:
Ghostly Childhood Memoirs

Thanksgiving Hen on a Chicken Shed:
Stories My Grandmother Told Me

*This book is dedicated to those paranormal investigators
who risk their lives for the sake of helping others.*

First publishing by CreateSpace Independent Publishing, 2015

All photos courtesy of the author

Table of Contents

INTRODUCTION

Why haunted collecting? This will forever remain the first question anyone asks me once they hear of my strange hobby. After all, this hobby proves to be a rather scarce one among people in the world. Most people think of it as too scary to comprehend. When most people think of a haunted item, especially a haunted doll which is mainly what the items in my collection are, they automatically think of those evil, possessed things which horror movies are made of. Or they might automatically think of real life items such as the Annabelle doll, a rag doll reported to have a demonic force attached to it, that is kept locked away in the Warren Occult Museum. Though items can be possessed by evil (and those items should not be tampered with except by those with the proper knowledge and experience to do so), not *all* of the haunted items in the world are automatically evil. It is a common misconception throughout the world today and is why I always get strange looks anytime someone hears of my own personal collection.

It is true that I have been in love with the paranormal field since early childhood when I first read *13 Alabama Ghosts & Jeffery* written by my favorite Alabama author, the late Kathryn Tucker Windham. All of her stories of the historical locations she visited that held legends of hauntings throughout centuries really fascinated me. It also did not help that I myself lived in a house built near ancient Native American burial ground. I grew up in a haunted neighborhood hidden away in the forests of the northwestern part of Jefferson County in Alabama. We kids shared all kinds of stories and legends that passed around our community over many years. I also experienced strange happenings in my own home such as doors slamming on their own, disembodied voices in the night, footsteps sounding in the hallway and on the stairs after everyone had retired to bed and even shadow figures rushing past through the moonlight that shined into our bedroom windows at night. Many of these stories including my own experiences were collected in my book *The Legends of Indian Narrows*.

In my adult years, I decided to go on my own paranormal adventures. It comes as no surprise that, not long after graduating from college, I became a paranormal investigator. Sometimes joined by friends and/or family, I traveled the southeast visiting haunted places from South Carolina all the way to Louisiana and even stretching beyond our region all the way to the coast of California. Some of the places I've investigated were the Sloss Furnaces in my own hometown of Birmingham, Alabama, Sturdivant Hall located in Selma, the Queen Mary docked out in Long beach, California, the beautiful Rice Hope Plantation out in Moncks Corner, South Carolina, and even deep down to the Louisiana bayous to such famous historic locations at Chretien Point Plantation in Sunset and the most haunted Myrtles Plantation in St. Francisville. I even spent multiple nights in some of these places (a few of the historic homes like the Myrtles and Rice Hope are open as bed and breakfast inns) to listen to the stories, research the paranormal happenings and experience them for myself.

Being fascinated by the paranormal, it now comes as no surprise, at least to me, that a pastime of collecting haunted items of my own awaited me in my future. Since 2013, I have collected haunted dolls, paintings and other items from around the country and even the world. Before that, I might have told you that the idea of me having haunted items in my own home was a little too close for comfort. However, the hobby has proved to be quite interesting and not as scary as I imagined.

Before I go further, I want to state a warning. Do you know those warnings that appear at the beginning of those daredevil type television shows that always state "Do not try this at home?" Well, I am stating the same. Haunted items are not things to be taken lightly or just for the sake of entertainment. I fear too many people might read this book, hear my story and on a whim might try to start collecting haunted items of their own because they enjoy those "ghost hunter" shows on television so much and, say, how cool would it be to actually have my own ghosts? Let me tell you, haunted collecting is a pastime that must be taken seriously and only by those knowledgeable in the paranormal, have experience in paranormal investigations and, bottom line, know what they are doing when it comes to this sort of thing! Trust me when I say: this is not the sort of thing you want to do because you are looking for a thrill! It's a very serious matter.

The following book is my own account of my experiences with the spirits of my haunted collection. Each and every spirit has been a delight to have in my home. Though some of the items look scary, the spirits attached to them exude the upmost respect for me and my care, and they show nothing but love for me. Believe me, that feeling is mutual. I've been asked many times how far I will go until I stop collecting. My answer remains the same: I will continue with it as far as it takes me.

Please enjoy this book. I am absolutely certain that my wonderful spirits are thrilled to have their stories shared and heard. Thank you for reading.

PART ONE:

Why On Earth Did I Decide To Get Into This?

The doll looked like an absolute angel. The sparkling blue eyes dazzled me. The little chubby cheeks turned my heart to mush. That amazing little smile made me long to make her mine. So what was the catch?

"She's haunted," Joanne advised me right up front on that spring day in May of 2013. An acquaintance of mine, Joanne decided to pass on a doll from her collection that she'd had for a short time during her life but now needed to find a good home for. The item was purchased from a woman who claimed to possess clairvoyance. At the time of purchase, Joanne received the warning about the doll which she now passed on to me. It once belonged to a little girl named Patty. The child, Patty, was only seven years old when she passed.

Sometime during the nineteen eighties, in what is believed to be somewhere in Michigan, Patty lived with her mother who practiced the age-old profession of prostitution. Mother wasn't very interested in having children. Because of her profession, and the fact that accidents do happen when we fail to practice the proper procedures of caring for ourselves, mother became pregnant and gave birth to a beautiful blonde child named Patty. A harsh life awaited the poor youngster. Her mother wanted nothing to do with her. The child was completely fatherless and had no one else to care for her. When she was old enough to get around, the child was left alone many nights to fend for herself while the mother went out to entertain clients sometimes until a very late hour and sometimes until the hours of dawn.

A neighbor felt sorry for Patty and gave her this particular porcelain doll. It was a baby doll in a crawl position with sparkling blue eyes and blonde hair, the same color of hair and eyes that Patty possessed. It wore a white bonnet with pink roses on each side, and a pink silk baby dress with pink silk pants to match. Its head, arms and legs were porcelain but the rest of the body was made of cloth. It was Patty's only toy and her prized possession. On those lonely nights, she clung to her doll and sought comfort from it. It stayed by her bed and she never let it out of her sight at home.

One fateful night, Patty's mother went on one of her all-night excursions leaving Patty in their apartment. Patty fed herself and prepared herself for bed. The urge for something sweet before bedtime overwhelmed her. Normally, her mother never bought any candy or desserts for her, but Patty wondered if she kept anything stashed away perhaps out of sight. Rummaging around in the kitchen, Patty came across what appeared to be small pieces of colorful candy. Her eyes bright with excitement, she opened the plastic bag containing the "candy" and tried a handful. Being only seven and having very little education, she had no way of knowing what she really swallowed.

Aside from being a prostitute, Patty's mother was also a big drug user. Often times she took payment of drugs instead of cash from her

Patty

clients. The plastic bag Patty came across that night contained some pills her mother had just recently acquired. The handful Patty swallowed proved too much for her tiny body. She went to bed ill and never woke up.

After Patty's death, the doll was given away and passed through random owners before it wound up in my friend Joanne's possession. The clairvoyant who sold the doll to Joanne advised her of the experiences prior owners of the doll reported when the doll resided in their homes. Each owner reported seeing the apparition of a small blonde girl in a white dress near the doll. Sometimes late at night, small footsteps could be heard from otherwise empty rooms after everyone in the household had retired to bed. The disembodied voice of a small girl was often heard talking, and sometimes even singing, near the doll.

Often times, the owners felt sharp tugs on their pants or shirt tails as if a child were standing next to them attempting to get their attention.

When Joanne purchased the doll, she didn't believe it to be haunted. She loved collecting dolls and other antiques and could not pass up on this adorable addition to her collection. She took it home, and the doll sat quietly in her collection. For the most part, she never heard much from the doll nor did she ever catch sight of a little girl spirit. However, something about the doll captured her interest as if she felt something really was with it, as if something were behind those sparkling blue eyes staring back at her. Sometimes she heard footsteps or what sounded like a small voice talking softly coming from the room where the doll sat on a shelf. However, upon entering the room, she never heard or saw anything and so chalked it up to her imagination.

Sometime later, due to personal reasons, Joanne decided she needed to downscale her collection, and Patty's doll was an important item she felt needed to go in the right hands. Because of my lifelong interest in ghosts and the paranormal, I seemed the right candidate for the job. As I mentioned before in the introduction chapter of this book, most people come away with the misconception that if an item is haunted, it's automatically evil. When Joanne told me of having a doll that was believed to be haunted, the first image that came to mind was Chucky from the *Child's Play* films standing in a doorway, knife brandished in his plastic hand, his mouth twisted back in a maniacal grin and shouting "Want to play?!!" Joanne quickly assured me that this was not the case. Patty's doll was very precious and probably may not even be haunted, but if it was, it never caused her any harm and actually she quite enjoyed having it in her home. Once Joanne showed me a picture of Patty Doll lying in that most adorable crawl position on her dining table, Patty's sparkling blue eyes won me over instantly.

So, I agreed to adopt Patty. I now welcomed my very first spirit daughter into my home. Although, I must admit at first I was very nervous at what I might hear or see in my home.

At the time I adopted Patty, I still rented a small townhome in Inverness, Alabama. Because Joanne lived out of town, Patty was shipped tightly in a box to my home. When I picked the box up from the post office and took it to my car, I swear I heard movement coming from within. When I got it home, I opened the box and took out Patty's doll. The minute I looked into her eyes in person, I felt like someone was there looking back at me. Small shivers like tingles ran through my body. I sat her down on the bed and, at the risk of feeling like the most foolish person in the world, began talking to her.

"Welcome, Patty, to your new home," I told her. "It is a pleasure to have you here."

Patty's first night in my home was a quiet night. I knew if the doll was really haunted the activity might not start right off the bat. I figured on it taking a few days for the little spirit to get used to me and her new home and feel comfortable enough to reveal herself to me. However, when I went to bed that night, I lay there in the dark gazing at that doll sitting on my dresser facing me. I could not help but wonder if I might wake up in the middle of the night to find a little girl standing next to my bed watching me. Would I feel someone crawling into my covers? Would I feel an icy hand come to rest on my arm? All kinds of thoughts went through my mind and made me slightly nervous. Still, I managed to drift off to sleep and had no problems.

On the second night after her arrival, I sat the doll on the bed and stepped back to take a picture with my digital camera. After downloading and inspecting the photo, I noticed a large white glowing ball hovering over the doll in the photo. I did not see this with my naked eyes when I took the photo. It only showed up in the photo itself. Most paranormal investigators calls this glowing ball an "orb" and say it possibly means that a spirit is attempting to manifest itself. Many skeptics chalk it up to dust or small bugs flitting about causing a reflection in the camera's flash. However, this was the only orb to show up in the photo and, coincidentally enough, was hovering directly over the head of Patty's doll.

A few weeks after the arrival of the doll into my home, I decided to try out an EVP (electronic voice phenomenon) session where I use a digital recorder to record myself asking questions. The theory is that digital recording devices can pick up on sounds and even voices that cannot be heard by the human ear. I stayed up late in the night and conducted a short session with the doll. The next day, when I played back the recording, I found I'd captured nothing. A little disappointed, I decided to keep trying regardless. Thankfully I did this because very soon my persistence would pay off.

About the third or fourth EVP attempting, I was sitting up with Patty's doll about one o'clock in the morning in the living room of my townhome with the doll sitting on a small table next to my recliner where I sat. I spent about ten minutes talking to her, asking her questions and even singing to her. Anything to try to get a response from this doll. Extremely tired by the end, I bid Patty good night, turned off the recorder and went on to bed.

The next morning, I played back this little ten minute session. No responses were captured and the recording reached the end. I was giving up hope when I noticed something strange at the very end of the recording. I heard an addition voice speak. My heart leapt! I played it back over and over. At first I was frightened, but the fright quickly turned to excitement. At the end of the recording, my voice is heard saying "Gotta go to bed now and go sleepy-pie." I know, that's very silly but considering how late the hour was at the time of the recording, my mind wasn't completely awake, and also I was speaking as if I were talking to a small child. Just as I reach to turn off the recording and let out a deep sigh, right behind me can be heard the softest, sweetest child's voice saying the word "Righteous!" The voice was that of a little girl, and it sounded so peaceful and angelic.

The excitement became overwhelming and I actually raced to Patty's doll, lifted her up into my arms, swung her around and cried "Thank you, Patty! Thank you, thank you so much for speaking to me!" I even plastered the poor doll's cheeks with big, sloppy kisses. Yes, this might sound strange, but again I was very excited to capture such clear evidence from my very first haunted item in my own home. I played the recording for my immediate family to hear. Needless to say, they were startled by it and got the creeps. I however maintained my excitement about my capture and even shared it with friends and the internet.

A few days later, I stood in the kitchen getting ready to leave for the day. I was at the kitchen sink washing a dish. I lived in the townhome alone so no one else was there but me. To my surprise, I felt two sharp little tugs on my shirttail on my right side. Turning and looking down, I saw nothing there. It felt as if a child had tugged on me to get my attention. Was it Patty? Thinking it might be, I spoke out to her and said hello to her. There was no response, but that would not be the last such experience. Every week, I experienced the tug whenever I was standing in my home alone. It happed in the daytime and at nighttime as well.

One Saturday, I sat home enjoying my day off from work snuggled up in my recliner watching television. I was having lunch and watching an episode of *I Love Lucy* as it was the best thing on at that time of the day. On the television, Lucy and Ethel were in the middle of one of their madcap predicaments. As the action grew sillier, right next to my recliner I heard the softest, sweetest giggle that sounded like a little girl. I immediately stopped and looked around. Of course, no one was there but me. At least, no one I could see. Thinking of how sweet the giggle sounded, I smiled in the direction where the noise came from and waived, hoping she saw me.

In the early summer of 2013, I published my first book, *Thanksgiving Hen On A Chicken Shed: Stories My Grandmother Told Me,* which was a short story collection about the stories my grandmother used to tell me about growing up in Alabama during the Depression. She passed away a few years before the book came out, and I did it as a tribute to her. When my copy of the book arrived from the publisher, I was overwhelmed to be holding my own first published book in my own hands. I raced to my office area in my bedroom and grabbed the digital camera. Setting it up on my dresser and starting the timer, I got in front of it and posed with my book to capture a picture. Right away, I posted it on my Facebook page for all my friends to see.

At the time, only a handful of people knew of my haunted doll Patty. One of my close friends saw the photo on Facebook and noticed something strange. He messaged me about it and asked me what it was. My curiosity on the verge of explosion, I quickly pulled up the photo on my computer and enlarged it to have a look at the anomaly he referred to. In the photo, over my right shoulder appeared a line of light. It had the shape of an arch coming up over my shoulder. One might think it just a flaw or reflection, however the hump seemed to be coming up from behind me, the bottom half of it blocked out by my shoulder. In fact, the shape appeared more like the outline of a small head peeking up over my shoulder. It even had the imagery of hair around it and a small ribbon on top.

"I think that's Patty wondering what you're up to there," my friend messaged me jokingly. I believe he was one hundred percent right.

After the picture I captured, I decided to start a page for Patty and her doll on Facebook where I could post and share my evidence. It also might help me locate some of Patty's former owners and hear their stories. Internet searches turned up no reports on Patty or her death, but her last name by then had been lost anyhow and pinpointing exactly what city she lived and died in, whether it was really in Michigan or not, proved impossible without more information about her. So, I started my page "Patty The Haunted Doll" on Facebook. I was surprised at how many "likes" the page got in a short amount of time, and how many others were out there collecting haunted dolls and items.

And So It Begins……

During the summer of 2013, growing quite tired of paying such a ridiculous amount of rent for my tiny townhome and feeling ready for a larger, more private space, I went house-hunting. In a short time, I located the perfect house in a small neighborhood out in the country in Shelby County and immediately made an offer. The offer was accepted, and I now owned my first home. I could not wait to move in. A large part of me hoped and expected that my little Patty ghost would become more active in better surroundings.

On the day of the move, I decided to take Patty Doll separately in my car away from the other boxes and items that would be taken for me by a moving company. Early that morning, I gently wrapped her doll in an afghan and placed it into a small box all of her own. All the while, I gently spoke out to Patty's spirit about our new home (something I'd already mentioned to her several times before leading up to the move) and told her it was time to go there. I asked her to please be sure to stay with her doll and come with me, that it was a joy to have her in my home and that I was already starting to think of her as my very own "spirit daughter." With that said, I carried Patty's box carefully to my car along with a small table for her, placed her box in the front passenger seat and her table in back, and left to take her to the new house.

Along the way down the highway, as I looked over at Patty's box, I could see her doll peeking out over the rim of the box, her face peering adorably out from the afghan, as if looking out the window at the beautiful outdoors zipping past us. When we arrived to the new house, I got her inside, set up her table then took her doll out from the box and afghan. Walking with the doll in my arms, I took her around the new house, showing her all the rooms and places she could go in, play in and just be herself. All the while, her doll seemed to smile up at me, her blue eyes sparkling with delight. I knew then that Patty's spirit had followed me to the new house. It made me very happy.

Not long after we moved in, I once again started feeling the tugs on my shirt. Patty was assuring me that she was still there with me. I heard disembodied sighs of content and heard small footsteps at night from time to time while I lay in my bed waiting to go to sleep. It gave me great comfort to know my spirit daughter was still hanging around for me. The experiences did not frighten me in the slightest. On the contrary, they made me smile and I slept quite peacefully at night.

It wasn't long before I started wondering if Patty was happy being the only spirit of the house. My new house was built in 2010 so was still very new. The prior owners were the only other people who ever lived there, and they were alive and well living off in Texas now. The land itself where the house and neighborhood were built had some Civil War history to it. However, the house itself did not feel haunted to me. During the days, I'd be at work all day and Patty was left to herself. I wondered if perhaps she might like a playmate. Was she lonely? Did she want a sister perhaps to spend time with and play with while the house sat empty during the day? I had the strongest feeling she wanted someone to play with and I could not overlook that feeling.

The thought occurred to me that, so far, I had not tried searches on the internet to determine if anyone out there might be a legitimate haunted collector who dealt extensively with such items and might be willing to "adopt" an item out. I began searching under "haunted items for adoption" and "haunted items for sale." I remained very leery about dealers online and auctions on reportedly haunted items because one never knows if 1) the person is lying and just trying to sell off a piece of junk while making a profit by claiming it's haunted or 2) the item in question might actually be haunted but by something evil or demonic and the seller was withholding that bit of information in order to get rid of the item quickly. Anyone thinking of adopting a haunted item into their home definitely must keep this in mind and be on the lookout. So, I chose the top dealers who came up on my searches and decided to ask around about them.

The dealer who showed up the most at the top of my search results was *AJ's Haunted Dolls*, a haunted doll adoption service run by doll collector and paranormal enthusiast Anjie Calvin Miller. I clicked for her website to check out what she had to offer. I must admit, the idea of a haunted doll adoption place made me scratch my head and brought a chuckle from my lips as I'm sure it would anyone reading this who did not know such people exist. Anjie had a nice yet limited selection of haunted dolls available. Several were child spirits just like Patty. Some of these children met tragic, untimely ends. Their stories touched me and made me long to embrace them all.

Deciding to check further, I went to Facebook. There are many paranormal group pages there with people who can give advice on such matters. I asked around about AJ and was given nothing but positive reviews. So, I decided to give her a shot first in my quest to find Patty a loving spirit sister.

Hello, Andrea!

While perusing AJ's haunted collection, one particular doll stood out to me. I mean, it practically screamed to my heart. The most beautiful and angelic doll came up on my screen with long strawberry blonde hair and a beautiful ruffled dress. Her blue eyes pierced me to the bone. AJ posted Andrea's story next to the picture, so I immediately read it.

The real Andrea was an eight year old child who came from St. Louis, Missouri. One summer day, she went for a swim in her next-door neighbor's pool. While she swam under water, her hair became caught in the pool's drain. She struggled to no avail. The other children at the surface and the parents near the pool failed to notice how long she'd been down until too late. Someone dove into the pool for her and managed to get her hair free, bringing her to the surface. CPR was performed on her but it was too late. Andrea passed away that day from drowning.

AJ took in Andrea's doll to her collection and kept it for about three years. During that time, she noticed activity with the doll. A child's footsteps were heard near it at night. AJ, being a clairvoyant, felt a presence with the doll and began studying it. Very quickly, she came into contact with Andrea's spirit. The spirit proved to be a very positive one and a sweet little girl at that.

My heart captured by the photo and story of this child and her doll, I immediately started the process of adopting her.

A few weeks later, Andrea's doll arrived on my doorstep. When I took her out of the box, I noticed her face held a very solemn expression. No smile graced her lips. She appeared not unhappy but just confused by her new surroundings. Trying not to feel like a fool, I began talking to Andrea and explaining who I was, why she was there and that this was now indeed her new home. I asked her to please make herself at home and feel free to be herself. In fact, I encouraged her to please show herself to me once she was ready but to take her time and just relax.

I took the doll to Patty and sat it next to hers. Instantly, I felt a warm breeze blow around me from the waist down. What felt like multiple little hands tugged on my shirt tail from either side, and I swear I heard little feet tapping as if two children were dancing in a circle around me.

After letting Andrea settle in for a few weeks, I decided to try the first EVP session with her. By this time, I'd acquired what paranormal investigators refer to as a "spirit box." This is a small hand-held radio designed to scan radio stations rapidly at five stations per second to create white noise suitable to help a ghost speak audibly. Using my new spirit box, I tried a session with Andrea and asked her to say her name. Quite clearly, I captured a little girl's voice saying "I'm Andrea." So clear was her voice that even a southern accent can be detected. Several seconds later, she said "Hello." The second response made me laugh because it did not sound like a "Hello" as in a normal greeting. It sounded more like "Hello" as in "Hello, dummy, you know my name already, so why are you asking me to say it." It sounded slightly sarcastic like a child might sound while rolling his/her eyes at you for saying something he/she thinks is dumb.

Not many weeks after, I tried a second session, this time with a video recorder going. At the end of this session, her little voice coming through did not make me laugh. This one instead captured my heart. Right as I was getting ready to end the session, her little voice came through shouting "Daddy" at me. It sounded like a squeal of excitement. So captured was my heart that, after thanking her so much, I leaned

Andrea

forward and planted a large kiss on the cheek of her doll. I could not help it. Just hearing her call me "Daddy" was too heartwarming for me not to react with love. Also captured in the video were several white orbs dancing around above the doll at the same time as that response was captured.

Another awesome thing happened with Andrea's arrival. She seemed to cause Patty to perk up and speak more to me as well. In every EVP session I did with Patty after Andrea's arrival, I always captured her voice saying something. When I told Patty I loved her, I captured a clear response from the ghost box: her little voice saying "I love you too." She was able to say her name for me as well and told me she was very happy in my home.

With the increase in EVP activity also came an increase in the physical activities. The sound of footsteps at night increased. On one occasion, I set up a video in my room while sleeping at night. Playing it back the next day, I captured Andrea's voice at one point humming a quick tune. Simultaneously, there is a small, sharp tug on the comforter at the foot of my bed as if someone stopped there to straighten it while passing through. Perhaps Andrea was checking on me while I slept.

A month or so after Andrea's arrival, I also saw the full-bodied apparitions of both girls! One night, while lying in my bed under the covers, my cat nestled next to me purring softly, I heard the sound of two sets of small footsteps coming from the kitchen located outside my bedroom door. I raised my head up and looked at the doorway. The sound of two little girls whispering softly reached my ears. My cat lying next to me perked up and stared at the door as well waiting to see what would happen next. To my ultimate surprise and shock, the most beautiful little head leaned in my doorway and looked in my bedroom at me. I could see her from her head to her shoulders. The rest was blocked by the doorway. She looked at me for a split second then darted back out, disappearing into the kitchen.

I knew right away who it was because she looked exactly like her doll right down to the same hair and similar dress. It was Andrea!

Part of me wanted to get up and go into the kitchen to see what I might find. But the logical part of me suggested I just stay put because most likely she'd disappeared and I'd be wasting my time. After all, those little ghosts don't usually wait around long once you've spotted them. I stayed there in bed with a big smile plastered on my face, excitement in my heart and still managed to drift off to sleep.

Not long after this encounter, I spotted the second apparition, this one in broad daylight. One Saturday afternoon, I was home doing some laundry. I just finished a load of towels, folded them and took them in the laundry basket into my master bathroom to the linen closet where I normally kept them. In the master bathroom, which branches right of from my bedroom, there is a long, tall mirror over a double vanity. The bathroom is like a long walkthrough with the vanity and mirror to the right and a shower stall and Jacuzzi bath to the left. At the end of the room is the linen closet and the water closet where the toilet is located. As I walked past that mirror with the laundry basket in hand headed toward the linen closet, something in that great mirror to my left caught my eye. It appeared someone was following right behind me. Someone awfully tiny and petite.

Turning my head to look fully at the mirror, I spotted the most adorable tiny little girl with shoulder-length blonde hair and wearing a white dress running happily along right behind me. She had her arms spread out and appeared like she was attempting to run past me to get ahead to the closet. I just knew right away from the descriptions I'd heard of prior owners of her doll who'd seen the little apparition that this indeed had to be my little Patty! Judging from her excited look, I believe she wanted to help me with that laundry!

I quickly turned to look behind me and greet her, but no one was there. I looked back in the mirror, and little Patty had disappeared. It was only a brief few seconds that I saw her, but it was a very exciting few seconds indeed. It was good to see Patty coming more and more out of her shell, communicating with me and most of all being happy.

As for Andrea, I also noticed a change in her doll. No longer did her face hold that blank, confused expression as when she arrived. Instead, her eyes now sparkled, and the design of her mouth, though it was porcelain and naturally impossible to move, had mysteriously changed on its own. Her lips were now curved into a happy smile.

And Then Comes Tammy…..

So, I believed once I'd adopted Andrea into my home, Patty had her a playmate and all was now right with the world. It proved exciting to have my two little ghost girls in my home. Theirs was a peaceful haunting and very much welcome. The idea of two haunted dolls in my very home made me feel special in an odd way. After all, I knew no one else in my family or any of my friends at the time who could claim having real haunted dolls in their possession. As far as I knew, I was done. Two little ghost girls were quite enough, or so I thought. Little did I know these two little ghost girls were only the beginning.

I still don't quite understand what pushed me to go back to AJ. One night, approximately two months after Andrea's arrival, I sat at my desk in my office at home doing the usual internet odds and ends: paying bills, checking Facebook and email and other such normality. It isn't unusual to be sitting at my computer in my office at home and feel the sensation of someone standing behind me watching over my shoulder with curiosity. Such was the case here. Suddenly, I felt the strongest push to go visit AJ's website for her haunted dolls. I asked myself why on earth I needed to do that because I had no plan whatsoever in adopting any further spirit children beyond the two I had already adopted. Still, the urging pushed its way through my heart and mind until I found myself typing in her website address.

On arrival to AJ's page, I noticed some new dolls added to her listing of available haunted item adoptions. One picture stood straight out to me instantly. The most beautiful porcelain doll with bright blue

Tammy

eyes and long brown braided pigtails stared back at me so innocently. I saw something sparkling in those eyes and knew right away I needed to click on her photo and read her story.

Her name was Tammy. Oddly enough, she came from St. Louis just like Andrea. Also like Andrea, the cause of death was drowning, however this drowning proved to be more sinister.

In life, Tammy lived alone with her mother in St. Louis sometime back during the seventies. Her father left them when Tammy was at a very early age so she had no memory of him, however Tammy lived a life of complete bliss with her mother. When Tammy was six, her mother remarried a man who loved Tammy and accepted her as his own daughter. Tammy's new stepfather also had two older daughters of his own from a prior marriage. These girls were in their teen years and none too happy about a new little stepsister coming into their home. Their father doted over Tammy which in turn caused the sisters to become quite jealous of her.

One evening, Tammy's stepfather decided to take her mother out on a date, Tammy's stepsisters were left in charge of babysitting her. Of course, the sisters held no excitement for this chore. Their jealousy at a boiling point, they plotted a nasty joke against her. They drew a tub of water. Calling to Tammy that it was time for her bath, they lured her into the bathroom. Grabbing her, they plunged her into the tub without waiting for her to even remove her clothes. Tammy struggled against them but her six-year-old petite little body proved no match to the two teenage girls. The two girls took turns holding Tammy under the water.

After a few minutes, Tammy struggled less and less against them. At one point, one of the girls continued holding Tammy under for a long time in order to really scare her. They really wanted Tammy to know who ruled the roost in their house. Eventually, Tammy stopped moving completely. The stepsisters let go of her and stepped back. Tammy made no motion to sit up out of the water.

Their jealous rage now turning to terror, the girls dragged Tammy from the tub. One of them felt for a pulse but found none. Neither girl knew how to perform CPR. They certainly did not want to call for help as they feared getting in trouble and even getting arrested for their fatal prank. Instead, they cooked up another plan. Taking off Tammy's wet clothes, they dried her off and placed her pajamas on her. Carrying her to her bedroom, they tucked her into her bed, closed her eyes for her and left her there to appear like she was asleep.

When the parents returned home, Tammy's mother peered into the bedroom door at the girl but, assuming she was asleep, left her alone. The next morning, when she tried to awaken Tammy, she realized the horrible truth. Tammy was dead.

After reading this story on AJ's page, I became completely interested in this doll and the spirit which haunted it. However, I had no plans of adopting any further haunted items other than the two I had. Going no further on the page, I turned off the internet and my computer. Turning off the light in my office, I started to bed. As I walked through the house to my bedroom, a feeling of desperation crept into my heart. The feeling grew stronger as I got closer to my bedroom door. Something pulled at me to go back. Something or someone literally screamed into my soul not to come to bed until I had adopted that doll. I cannot explain this other than the power of suggestion. I knew it had to be from Andrea. After all, she had come from AJ's home as well. Perhaps she wanted me to adopt Tammy. Did she give me the suggestion to go look at AJ's page that night to begin with? I now believe so.

Feeling very restless and knowing the feeling would not go away on its own, I turned and went straight back to my office and to my computer. Going to AJ's website, I immediately put in the request to adopt Tammy. Later on after making the request, I contacted AJ via email and asked her about the doll. I told her about the strong pull I had to adopt Tammy. Being new to the haunted collecting world, I did not understand how the spirits worked. AJ informed me that, when Andrea was in her home for those three years, her doll did sit in very close proximity to Tammy's doll. Perhaps the spirit girls became friends, even spirit sisters, during the time they spent together. Tammy had been in AJ's collection the exact same three years as Andrea. I needed no further convincing than this. Call it a coincidence as you will, but I believe Andrea wanted her sister to come join her in her new home.

Not long after Tammy came into my home, I began hearing strange noises at night coming from my master bathroom near my bedroom and close to where I kept her doll. It sounded like the cabinet doors banging open and shut as if someone were looking through them in search of something or just simply at play. One late night, I was awakened by the sound of the faucet of that bathroom sink turning on. The sound of the running water roused me up. At first, I thought perhaps my cat Maddie was messing around in there and perhaps, using her paw, had batted the faucet knob around causing the water to turn on. However, as I sat up in bed, my hand came to rest on her fur as she lay there right next to me on the bed waking up from her own slumber. I hurried into the bathroom to see what caused the water to turn on. Before I could enter the bathroom door, the faucet shut off. I turned on the lights but saw nothing out of place. For a few seconds, I stood there looking around waiting to see what might happen next. When nothing happened, I turned the light off. Heading back to my bed, I heard the faucet switch on and off really quick behind me. I laughed as I realized this had to be one of my little spirit daughters playing around. On recounting this to AJ, she confirmed that Tammy's spirit had often times played around in her bathroom as well while the doll resided in her house.

One evening as I was heading to bed, I said goodnight to my little spirits as I normally do. I decided to try capturing an EVP so I placed my digital recorder next to Tammy's doll. I said goodnight to her then left the recorder running for several minutes. Eager to hear what I might have captured, I shut off the recorder and took it into the kitchen where I plugged in my ear buds and listened to what I'd just recorded. On the recording, right after I say goodnight to Tammy and tell her I love her, a small child's voice could be heard as if coming right behind me. The voice said "Daddy?" as if calling out to me, and it had the sweetest tone to it. What is even more amazing is that fact that, when I was standing there next to Tammy's doll while saying goodnight to her, the door to the master bathroom stood right behind me. Judging by the acoustics of the voice on the recording, it sounded as if she was standing in the bathroom calling out to me. This capture definitely excited me and I played it back several times to listen before I finally got to bed. The fact that she called me "Daddy" certainly captured my heart and made me very happy.

So, here I now was what my friends in the haunted collecting world call a "spirit daddy." As far as I could tell, the spirits of three little girls now resided in the walls of my home. An "average joe" might certainly cringe at the idea. Not me. On the contrary, I welcomed the idea. The girls were a complete delight, their haunting most peaceful and pleasant. They never did anything to frighten me or make me believe I might be in harm's way. I continued to enjoy their presence with me and tried to communicate with them on a daily basis.

Each week, I held an EVP session with each girl. I took turns with them and gave them each a chance to say anything they needed to. In each session, I set up my digital video cameras, my digital recorders, my spirit box and a couple of EMF detectors (electromagnetic field readers which paranormal investigators believe can detect the presence of spirits when they attempt to manifest) and asked a series of questions to see if I might capture a response. In the videos, I captured several orbs and misty images. I also took still photos with my digital camera that also captures these anomalies. In some sessions, the girls remained quiet on the EVP side, but in others they answered my questions and continued to say my name or call me "Daddy" which still delighted me.

Almost every day, I'd have at least once instance where I'd feel a small hand come to rest on my arm while I was sitting down on the couch in my great room or standing in the kitchen. Sometimes, my kitchen chairs moved around on their own as if children were sitting there playing and left them pushed out. Small footsteps continued to be heard at night and the sound of giggles floated gently on the air. I even heard the occasional relaxed sigh come from behind me when no one was around.

Patty's Facebook page was extended to being called "Patty and Andrea, The Haunted Dolls" so that I could include information and activity on all of my girls, including Tammy and any others that might be added later. In a short amount of time, the "likes" on the page increased by a few hundred. It was amazing how many others shared an interest in haunted dolls and other items of the paranormal.

As the activity continued in my home, not only did I keep posting on the Facebook page about it to keep my followers informed, but I also decided to keep a written journal about my experiences so I could keep a solid record to reflect back on. The next section of this book contains actual entries from that journal.

PART TWO

A Journal of Paranormal Activity

October 4th, 2013

This week presented a few nice experiences. Earlier this week, I was just walking away from Patty's doll when I felt a small hand touch mine. It felt like Patty's spirit was walking with me and perhaps wanted to hold hands.

Today, when I got home, I went into the bedroom (where I keep Patty and Andrea's dolls while I am gone during the day) and found Patty's afghan lying off her table on the floor as if it something knocked it off. This is a lovely blue and white afghan that Patty's doll sits on for comfort on the table. It is normally folded up underneath her doll. Her doll still sat in its normal position on the table. How did the afghan fall to the floor if it was under the doll and the doll was still sitting safely on the table? I keep the bedroom door closed during the day while I am gone so that my cat Maddie cannot get into the room and hurt the dolls. No one else was here in the house. A short time later, I walked back into the bedroom and found the door that leads from the bedroom to the laundry room cracked open where it was completely closed a few minutes before.

My favorite experience happened back in early September of this year before I purchased this journal but I wanted to go ahead and record it today to be sure it is documented. It was just a few night after the arrival of Andrea's doll. I'd just turned off the lights in the bedroom and settled into my bed. No sooner than my head came to rest on the pillow that I felt a small hand…..a child's hand with tiny fingers….start to caress my hair on the left side of my head. Then, if that wasn't surprising enough, I felt a small form slide up next to me in the bed as if a small child had just eased under the covers and curled up next to me. As shocking as it was, I was not scared in the slightest. Instead, I smiled in the darkness, laughed and said, "I love you girls!" I then drifted off into a sound, peaceful sleep.

It was an incredible experience. These little spirits are amazing and I love them. I call them "spirits" for I think calling them "ghosts" is not proper. Spirits is a better name for them and sounds more respectful. I do love and respect these little spirit girls….my own adopted spirit daughters!

October 9th, 2013

Came home today to a nice spooky surprise. I've made one of the spare rooms in my new house into a library. During the day when I am gone to work, I keep the doors to the library and to my office closed to keep the kitten out. When I left the library room this morning, closing the door behind me, everything in that room appeared in order. On returning home this afternoon, I opened the door to the library to find a book lying on the floor as if someone had been lying there earlier reading it and left it there. It was one of my old children's books I owned when I was a kid. The name of this book is *The Great Book of Giant Stories*. It's a picture book with funny stories about bumbling giants and was one of my favorites as a child.

After I adopted Andrea, AJ warned me that Andrea loved to read books and sometimes will leave books lying around. I believe this may have been Andrea in the library reading my book! I have of course invited both her and Patty to enjoy the library and my books anytime they please, and I dearly hope I find some more activity in there.

October 16th, 2013

Caught some amazing pictures tonight which I posted on the girls' Facebook page. The first one caught an anomaly near my bean bag chair in the library room. The chair sits right next to the same place where I found my children's book lying on the floor last week.

The second photo was even more amazing. I snapped a picture looking into the laundry room. I've noticed my cat Maddie staring in there like she sees someone or something in there. Apparently, she really is seeing something. In the photo, I captured a hazy misty standing in front of the closed door that leads out from the laundry room into my bedroom where the dolls stay mostly. The misty shape is the height of a child and was almost a distinct figure of a little girl. I think one of the girls was attempting to manifest! I do hope I see one or both of the girls one day and have asked them to please show themselves to me when they are ready.

October 19th, 2013

Caught great EVP with the spirit box and my camcorder in the wee hours of the morning. Over the spirit box, Patty said her name for me and then said "Hi....Kevin." Captured this on my voice recorder as well.

Later on, I let my camcorder run in my bedroom while I slept. Later this morning, when I played it back, I captured the sound of a little girl's voice humming. At the same time, the comforter on my bed was given a sharp tug at the foot of the bed. The camera did capture this as well. Excellent evidence of my precious spirit girls!

October 22nd, 2013

I had Andrea's doll sitting next to me on the sofa tonight. I was watching a movie when suddenly her doll leaned my way all by itself and let her head come to rest on my shoulder! Absolutely amazing!

Halloween Night, 2013

Did an EVP session using the spirit box shortly after midnight. One of the girls said "Hi" and also said "Cheese!" while I was taking pictures. Such adorable voices. Held the session in my bedroom where the dolls usually stay. Captured some very nice anomalies in my photos taken during the session as well.

November 1ˢᵗ, 2013

Felt one of the girls snuggle up next to me again in the bed shortly after I shut out the bedroom lights and turned in for the evening. It felt like cold air pressing up next to me under the covers. It's a very interesting experience. These girls never cease to amaze me.

November 6ᵗʰ, 2013

This morning, as I was leaving for work, I said goodbye to the girls as I normally do. I picked up Patty's doll and hugged it. It suddenly vibrated in my arms! Not the first time this has happened. Both her doll and Andrea's doll do this from time to time when I hug them. Neither doll has anything electrical or mechanical inside it that would cause it to vibrate. I love it!

Tonight, I heard Maddie, my cat, whine from the entryway to the library. I went to check on her and found her sitting there looking around. She seemed to be okay. The door to the library was wide open as I had left it earlier. I did not look into the library itself but turned and walked away. Just moments later, I returned to the library to find the door most of the way closed where I had left it wide open before. The two windows inside were closed tight and the door itself is not easy to move without a good push. I think one of the girls was in there enjoying the books and, when Maddie started in, closed the door to keep her out so she wouldn't disturb them. Maddie probably did not like their not wanting her to come in, which is most likely why she whined.

I went the rest of the way into the library and found everything in proper order. Nothing had been moved, or at least did not appear to have been moved. I took some pictures of the room but nothing out of the ordinary showed up in the pictures.

I had both dolls out on the sofa with me this evening when all of this transpired. Maddie eventually climbed up on the sofa and laid down next to them. I got my camera and took a photo. In the picture, a nice little white anomaly, a little ball of light, appears next to them. Very interesting indeed!

November 9th, 2013

Last night, as I drifted off to sleep, the cat Maddie lying next to me on the bed, we listened to movement in the bedroom and what sounded like little footsteps walking around the bed. Even Maddie lay there with her ears perked up with interest listening to the noises.

This morning, I lay in bed after waking up and listened to the room around me. Once again, the little footsteps could be heard, this time in my bathroom, followed by the sound of something being moved. I don't know what was being moved around in there. I got up to check it out, and nothing appeared out of place when I went into the bathroom just moments after the sound stopped. I also caught a glimpse of movement in the doorway, but whatever it was quickly disappeared.

November 11th, 2013

Last night, I lay on the bed with Andrea and Patty's dolls sitting in front of me. I talked to them and spent time with them. While I was talking to them, I felt cold, invisible little fingers caress my hands. It was a sweet, remarkable experience.

November 14th, 2013

I finally *saw* one of the girls last night. After I shut out the lights, I lay down in bed and the cat lay down next to me purring away. Out in the kitchen, which is right outside my bedroom door, I hear little footsteps, some sort of shuffling noise and then the voices of little girls talking barely above a whisper.

I looked over at the bedroom door just in time to see a little girl poke her head in the doorway, look at me and then quickly duck back out. I am not quite sure which one it was because she was too fast, but she had long hair, was petite, appeared to be wearing a dress and was about 7-8 years old. She appeared slightly transparent.

Part of me wanted to get out of the bed and go in there, but I decided not to disturb them and stayed where I was. The noises ceased shortly after the apparition ducked out. I did also feel a warmth at the foot of my bed as if someone had just lay an electric blanket across the bed down there over my feet. It stayed warm like that until I drifted off to sleep.

I believe the girl I saw was Andrea! For one thing, the little girl looked exactly like Andrea's doll, and the story is that when Andrea was alive the doll was bought for her because it looked like her. Another thing is that, earlier that night before bed, I had both Patty and Andrea's dolls on the sofa with me while watching television. The whole time, Andrea's doll seemed to want to lean over closer and closer to me with this little smile playing across her lips. I finally took her and held her in my lap for the rest of TV time. I think she has a crush on her spirit daddy! Haha!

November 17th, 2013

Last night, I did an EVP session with the girls using a camcorder and the spirit box. I captured Patty laughing at a comment I made about my cat Maddie being so hyper that she literally bounces off the walls. Patty's little laugh was too adorable for words. I heard it live from the spirit box even as I was recording the session. After I heard it, I said to her "That is the cutest laugh." To which she replied, "Yeah!" I was holding her doll in my arms at the time all of this happened. The camcorder captured the evidence beautifully!

November 18th, 2013

When I left for work this morning, I made sure to turn off all the lights in the house before leaving like I always do every morning. I leave the blinds slightly cracked open so sunlight will come in. I kiss Patty and

Andrea goodbye then tell the kitty Maddie goodbye, then I leave for work.

Later in the evening after work, I stopped for a quick errand on the way home. Because of the sun setting earlier this time of year, it was already getting dark when I got home. After I parked the car in the garage, I entered the house, and of course Maddie was waiting right inside the door for me. I noticed that it wasn't pitch black in the house like I thought it would be, and there was a reason. Going the rest of the way through the door, I noticed a light coming from the kitchen. The overhead kitchen light was turned on!

I think my sweet little girls turned the light on for me and for Maddie because it was getting dark outside and I wasn't home yet. After all, I needed a light to see my way into the house. What precious little sweet-peas they are for looking out for their daddy and kitty. No one else could have possibly done it because the house was all locked up and the alarm set. I am the only living soul who lives there and no one else had been in the house today.

November 19th, 2013

I was here in my office at home working on the computer before bedtime. I got out my EMF detector planning on taking it into the bedroom to spend some time with Patty and Andrea. I already had the EMF switched on. As I left the office to go out through the great room, the EMF goes off in my hand spiking at 3 and 4 on the digital screen. These are fairly high spikes for EMF. I stopped in my tracks. The EMF detector spiked on for a second then stopped. I stepped further into the great room and nothing happened. When I turned back in the direction of the office, the EMF spiked again at 3 and 4.

I moved back toward the office. The EMF spiked again. To the right of my office door sits a guest bathroom. The EMF seemed to spike more toward that direction. The door had been wide open earlier but now it was partially closed. I pushed it the rest of the way open....and behold, there was a pile of toilet paper on the floor! The roll of paper hanging next to the toilet had been completely unraveled from the roll and then clawed into shreds.

Recently, I have had issues with my cat Maddie going into the bathroom and playing maliciously with the toilet paper roll, completely wasting some. I have been attempting to train her so she will not do this but it's taking a good bit of work to get through to her. I believe these EMF spikes I received were my little girls leading me to the guest bathroom so I would see the mess kitty made. Special thanks to the sweet dumplings for making me aware right away that kitty had been a bad girl again.

November 22nd, 2013

Held an EVP session with the girls. Andrea set off my EMF detector with great excitement. I think she wants to tell me something though she didn't voice it.

Patty talked to me and told me through the spirit box that her favorite ice cream flavor is "orange....vanilla," in her own words. How adorable!

November 26th, 2013

Maddie the cat was racing around the house, running in circles then lunging at air like she was trying to catch something…or someone…I couldn't see. Really amazing and fun to watch.

Last night as I lay in bed, I felt a small hand caress my cheek. I think Andrea is happy with me for adopting Tammy, her spirit sister who is also coming from AJ's home. Tonight, I had Andrea's doll out with me sitting on the couch. I got up to play with Maddie for a while to wear out the blasted hyper energy she seemed to filled with, and suddenly the sweetest smell came floating around me. It smelled like children's shampoo or powder. I absolutely loved it! I can't wait to see what happens when Tammy gets here.

When I caught that sweet scent, I did take some photos in the room. They captured several large, bright orbs.

December 2nd, 2013

This past Thanksgiving weekend provided some great experiences. Late Saturday evening, I was walking with a basket of clean towels into the master bathroom. I crossed the bathroom headed toward the linen closet to put them away. There is a large mirror over the double vanity in that bathroom. As I walked past it, I noticed in the reflection a little blonde girl (it had to be Patty) following right behind me. She looked to be seven years old, the same age as Patty, and she was so cute and tiny. She wore a white sleeveless dress and the tips of her blonde hair were in curls. She was walking very fast behind me with her arms outstretched like she was hurrying to help me with the towels.

When I turned and looked behind me, no one was there. I looked back in the mirror, and the little girl was gone. I am so happy to have seen Patty. I have now seen both of my little spirit girls and am very excited about it.

The next evening, I sat in the middle of my couch in the great room watching TV. Both Patty and Andrea's dolls were out with me sitting to my right at the end of the couch. Maddie jumped up on the couch and started staring at me with her eyes wide. All of a sudden, I felt a small finger touch my shirt over my chest. At the same time, Maddie looked directly at my chest as if she saw it there. I feel the little finger start tracing down my chest, and simultaneously Maddie's gaze followed down my chest as if watching the unseen finger move. Suddenly, the feeling went away. This was very remarkable!

We still await Tammy's arrival.

December 3rd, 2013

Tammy has finally arrived tonight and in the eeriest way. She was delivered by UPS. Normally, they deliver by sundown however today that was not the case.

At ten o'clock tonight, I was sitting on the couch with Maddie and Patty's doll watching some late TV. From outside my house came the sound of a motor as if a large truck pulled up in front. I muted the television and got up to check the front of my house. As I proceeded toward the front door, I heard a thumping sound outside. I reached the door and opened it just in time to see a UPS truck speed off into the night.

Sitting just outside the door was the box from AJ containing little Tammy's doll. I've never heard of UPS delivering that late before, and it was curious how he dumped the box and fled instead of knocking like he normally does. He was in quite the hurry to leave.

In any case, we are so happy that Tammy has arrived. Especially Andrea!

December 5th, 2013

Spent the evening with Tammy. I think she is already warming up to her new surroundings. After turning off the TV for the evening and returning to the bedroom, right after I placed her doll back on the dresser, I saw a small shadow outside the bedroom doorway going across the kitchen wall as if a small figure had just entered from there into my bedroom. The kitchen light was out and the light spilling across the wall from my bedroom is what caught the shadow.

I stepped out into the kitchen just to have a look but found nothing there. Upon inspection, I determined that, for a shadow to cross the wall, someone would have had to walk into the bedroom or at least in front of the bedroom door, so I know it wasn't me as I was already all the way into the bedroom and away from the door where light was being cast. Very interesting stuff. I shall try an EVP session with Tammy in the next few weeks. First, I want her to continue settling in to her new home and getting used to me. I have a feeling she likes me already.

December 9th, 2013

Went to bed and the cat joined me as usual. We were lying there with the lights off in the house preparing to go to sleep. From the kitchen comes the sound of one of the chairs being dragged slightly across the floor. The next morning, when I entered the kitchen, I did notice one of the chairs pulled away from the kitchen table at an angle as if someone had pulled it out to sit down.

Tammy is warming up to me now. I have been able to get her to respond to me with light knocks on the wall in response to questions. I hope to learn more about her soon. We will try an EVP session in the near future.

December 23rd, 2013

Tammy spoke a little in our first EVP session this past Friday night. She responded to one question clearly through the spirit box. The question was "What is your favorite color?" Her response was, "Yellow."

Activity has seemed to pick up a little in the house. Last night I awoke around two in the morning to a sound coming from the master bathroom. It sounded like the roll of toilet paper hanging on the wall was being spun loudly and rapidly. At first, I assumed it was the cat playing around in there…until I sat up and found her lying on the bed right next to me sound asleep!

Getting out of bed, I went into the bathroom to check it out. The toilet paper roll appeared untouched. Nothing appeared out of place.

December 26th, 2013

I was in the kitchen putting some things away and getting ready to turn in for the night. I turned around toward the bedroom doorway just in time to see the tail-end of a little dress disappearing into the bedroom as if a little girl had just hurried in there. I walked over and looked into the bedroom but of course no one was in there. A little while later, I heard a little girl talking in there but I couldn't make out what she was saying.

No matter how many experiences I have with these girls, each and every episode never ceases to amaze me. Can't wait to see and hear more!

January 3rd, 2014

Went to bed for the night. As I lay there, I felt three distinct little forms lie down at the end of the bed near me feet. Two lay down one on each side of me, and the third actually laid across my legs. Felt like my little angels were joining me on the bed for the night.

January 4th, 2014

Recorded a short video on my smartphone tonight just after doing an EVP session with Tammy. Caught some excellent anomalies. Some came from Tammy's doll and there were even some coming from Patty and Andrea's dolls. The best orb was a large one that flew directly at my camera from Tammy's doll. Very stunning video capture. I think I will start using my smart phone to video as it seems to capture more activity than the camcorder.

PART THREE:

The Rest of My Haunted Collection

With the wonderful, amazing experiences I was having with my first three haunted items, it stood to reason that I simply had to collect more. The urge to study more items became too great to pass up. So, over the next year, I collected a total of seventy haunted items which I brought into my home. Most were haunted dolls with the spirit of children attached to them. Some had teenagers and adults. There were other items as well, such as paintings, an antique cobbler's tool and even a doll carriage.

In this section are the stories of the some of the most amazing items in my haunted collection.

HILDA

Around the late fall of 2013, I received a message online about an item a young woman attempted desperately for some time to get rid of. The woman, whose name shall remain anonymous, resided in California and had posted an auction numerous times for an antique painting she wished to sell. I shall call her Luna for the purpose of telling this story. The painting was a copy, not an original, but was still at least over one hundred years old with its original antique black wooden frame. According to the message I received, the woman had tried for several months to auction it off on Ebay however could find no bidders. A link to the current auction was included. My interest peaked, I checked out the auction.

The auction page on Ebay included a few photos of the painting. The portrait was of a young Victorian woman no older than her early twenties posing with her head turned slightly as if she were looking off to the side at something pleasant. She had a slight smile on her face and wore a dress which appeared very Victorian. Her light brown hair was held up in a bun on the back of her hair, and her skin gave off a porcelain complexion. She was quite beautiful. Luna did not know who the woman in the portrait was or the name of the artist. According to her listing, Luna purchased the painting from a curiosity shop in San Francisco. The owner of said shop did not speak English but seemed very anxious that Luna look at the painting and buy it. Luna loved the portrait for its beauty, decided it would look very beautiful hanging up on her dining room wall at home and decided to buy it.

Only a few weeks after she hung the picture in her home, Luna began experiencing some strange goings-on. The voice of a woman was heard coming from the dining room when Luna was all alone in her

The portrait haunted by Hilda

house. She'd never heard this before. On checking out the dining room, she found no one there. Only the painting of the mystery woman smiling at her. This happened on several occasions. The voice was always soft and Luna could never quite tell what it was saying. It almost sounded musical.

A month or so after this, Luna was sitting in her dining room having dinner with a friend. Her friend kept looking at the painting and asked Luna about it. She told Luna that the painting gave her a strange feeling, almost like the woman in the painting was real and watching her. As the friend continued to keep her eye on the painting, she noticed the woman in the painting began to move slightly. In one instance, the woman was smiling bigger. In another instance, her head was slightly turned more toward where she was facing forward. Luna observed the painting and noticed these changes as well. Had she been alone, she might have thought herself crazy or seeing things, but her friend was with her and saw the same eerie changes in the painting.

After that, whenever Luna or guests to her home entered the dining room, they always noticed the woman in the painting had changed facial expressions. Sometimes she smiled, and other times she looked melancholy. Sometimes she might be leaning forward more where other times she sat up straight. This gave Luna a very uneasy feeling about having the painting in her home, and she pondered the possibility of selling it. One evening, Luna went into the dining room to turn off the light on her way to bed. As usual, she glanced up at the painting. This time, the woman in the painting had turned her head to face straight ahead and stared directly at Luna! This was the final straw in the haystack of Luna's spooky experiences. She fled the room, and the next day when it was light, she returned and took the painting down.

Luna completely removed the painting from her home. She took it to a storage room that her friend owned and kept it there while she busied herself in an attempt to sell it. Ebay seemed like her best option so she posted an auction for the painting. Unfortunately, the listing of a haunted painting on Ebay seemed to push possible buyers away rather than draw them.

When I came to the auction page, I immediately contacted the seller. I explained to her that I was a paranormal investigator turned haunted collector and wanted very much to take that painting off her hands. She was more than delighted. By this point, she wanted rid of the painting so badly that she let me have it at a very low cost which mainly consisted of shipping to get it from California to my home in Alabama.

The day the painting arrived to my home, which was around Thanksgiving of 2013, I came home from work to find the large flat box waiting for me outside my front door. I hurried it in and took the painting out. Immediately, a cold draft blasted from the box as I slid the painting out. The painting itself was quite cold as well. Bringing out my EMF detector, I was able to get hits on the detector from the painting itself and the area immediately around it. I felt confident whatever spirit had attached to it had followed the painting faithfully to my home. With pride, I hung the painting right way in the great room of my house for all to see.

A few weeks after the painting's arrival, I decided to try an EVP session with it just like I did with the haunted dolls. Using a spirit box, digital camera and voice recorder, I spent about thirty minutes one night around midnight asking questions toward the painting, requesting that the spirit tell me who she was and where she was from. I asked for cause of death and to let me know why the spirit was attached to this painting.

When I played back the video the next morning, I was both excited and chilled when I found I'd captured responses. The voice of a rather young woman, possibly in her twenties like the woman in the painting, answered a few of my questions. At the point of the recording where I asked for a name, the voice responded with "Hilda." When I asked for a last name, it responded with what sounded like "Michaelsford." When I asked for a cause of death, the chilling response was "You'd have to find my body." From this response, I gathered the poor woman probably does not know how she died. Perhaps it was sudden, even a surprise, like an accident or even someone sneaking upon her and murdering her. This is the feeling I got from listening to the voice. At the end of the recording,

I told her how beautiful her painting was, how happy I was to have it in my home and that I thanked her for being there. Her voice responded quite pleasantly with "Thank you so much."

Some physical activity has occurred around the painting. Orbs have been caught on the video entering and exiting the painting. I managed to catch an orb flying out of the painting on video at the same time I captured one of the EVP's mentioned above. Another occurrence had to do with the sofa that sits right under this painting. There are two throw pillows for the sofa, and one sits on each side. One evening, I lay on the sofa while watching television there in the great room. I sort of tossed the two pillows to the side while I lay there. As the night wore on and I grew sleepy, I turned off the television and retired to bed, leaving the pillows tossed aside.

The next morning, I walked through to great room on my way out to work. I noticed the pillows still tossed to the side. I expected company later that evening but decided not to fool with any straightening up until I got home from work that afternoon. I said a goodbye to Hilda as I normally do when leaving for the day, then I left. When I returned home that afternoon and entered the great room, to my surprise the two pillows were back in their respective locations, one on each side of the couch, and both angled in such a fashionable way that whoever straightened them had taken so much pains that they had even stepped back to inspect their work and took the effort to angle those pillows in a lovely display. No one else lives in my house or was there that day. I highly doubt my small cat was strong enough or smart enough to drag those pillows up there and position them.

An idea occurred to me suddenly as I looked at those pillows. I stole a glance up at Hilda's painting and noticed the woman was smiling slyly. In my heart of hearts, I do believe it was Hilda's spirit who placed those pillows lovingly back into place and positioned them for me. Being the proper lady she is, I am sure she did not want the great room in any disorder before company came. Happily, I thanked her aloud multiple times for straightening those pillows for me.

To date, I have not been able to find out much about the painting as far as who owned it prior, where it came from or anything about Hilda Michaelsford. Though the name is unique, internet searches have provided no information on any such person. An odd coincidence however did come to my attention. There is a copy of Hilda's painting hanging in the very haunted Myrtles Plantation in Louisiana. Just a coincidence? I contacted the Myrtles to inquire about their copy. Theirs is just a copy as well and they have no information other than a prior owner of the plantation bought it at an auction. The whereabouts of that auction are unknown. So, for now, Hilda remains a mystery.

MACI

The fourth haunted doll I received in my collection brought a surprise that still has me reeling to this day. A very dear friend of mine named Sherry Richardson, otherwise known as Doll Haven, adopted out a doll to me that was allegedly haunted by a precious little seven year old girl named Maci. I felt my three spirit daughters wanted more playmates to join the family, so when Maci became available for adoption, I could not resist, especially after hearing her story.

Maci lived in a bad home with a very abusive father. He often beat her and then, to prolong her punishment, forced her into her bedroom closet where he locked her in until he felt the punishment was complete. Maci spent many hours locked away in that dark closet. Her fear of the dark grew more and more each day until she refused to sleep without a light. Unfortunately, on one of those days when her father was too drunk to control himself, Maci was beaten so severely that she died from her injuries. It was uncertain if the doll she now haunted actually belonged to her, but she definitely chose to haunt the doll because it looked so much like her when she was alive. It had long blonde braids and bright blue eyes just like she once possessed in life.

When Maci arrived to my home, I instantly felt a strong positive energy radiating from her even from the moment I lifted her doll out of the box. I placed the doll in the middle of the sofa and welcomed her to her new home. Switching on the television, I turned and went into the kitchen to discard the box. When I came back to the great room just seconds later, the doll had moved from the middle of the couch over to the right side of the couch where it leaned against one of the throw pillows resting against the arm of the couch. The doll was turned in such a way that her eyes were directed straight at the television. A smile played across her lips.

Doll Haven advised me that Maci did not like the dark and to be sure to keep her doll near light. I decided to keep her doll in my bedroom with the other three. Maci's was placed on a small table right next to the bedroom window where plenty of sunlight shined in during the day. At night, I left a nightlight on in the bathroom. Her table sat close to the bathroom door as well so this gave her a little light. Just a few weeks later, after letting her settle in, I brought Maci's doll out to the great room around midnight and began an EVP session with the ghost box which I captured on video. She immediately gave me some responses to my questions without hesitation.

When I asked her if I were taking good care of her, she answered clearly and loudly, "Yes…you are!" She described herself as having blonde hair and blue eyes. Her final response to me brought chills to my bones. I asked her what city she was from. She replied, "Adamsville."

Maci

The reason this chilled me so is because Adamsville is the city where I grew up in Alabama. Could this be Maci's hometown as well? The next morning, I played that EVP several times while listening and pondering. Realization flooded over me as to who this spirit just might be.

If you've read my ghost story collection titled *The Legends Of Indian Narrows: Ghostly Childhood Memoirs*, you are familiar with a particular story within it about a small girl who once lived in my old neighborhood. She had horrid parents who were drug and alcohol users. They severely abused her for any little mishap or anytime they felt she got in their way. One night, they abused her to the point of death. With no remorse, they tossed her into the closet and left her for dead. After police discovered what happened, the parents were arrested and taken away. For a long time after, that little girl's spirit was said to haunt that home. Even after it burned down some time later, her spirit was still seen in and around the property until eventually the sightings died down and her story faded to the wind.

That little girl's name was said to be Cami. If you notice, the name is eerily similar to Maci, including the fact that the exact same letters are used in the way each name is spelled, just in a different arrangement. Could this spirit be the same one now haunting the doll in my possession?

Two months later, I held another EVP session with Maci. Again, I held it in the great room around midnight. I captured this session on video as well. The EVP captured via the ghost box proved much eerier than the first. The voice of an unexpected guest came through.

I was sitting quietly holding Maci's doll in my arms and looking around the room waiting to see if anything would happened. Over the spirit box, a voice hissed through. It was male and sounded angry. It said, "Maci…..get in your closet!" About five seconds later, Maci's voice was heard responding with a loud "No!" Several seconds later, I asked Maci if she were happy living with me. The same voice that shouted "no" earlier now responded with "Yes!"

The next morning, I played back the recording over and over. It baffled me how clear this EVP sounded. At first, I wondered if the spirit of Maci's father inhabited the doll as well. However, I now believe she was only giving me a voice from her past to confirm what had happened to her. After all, I have felt nothing but positive vibes from the doll. In my heart, I do believe Maci is indeed the same girl as Cami from the story back in my old neighborhood. How coincidental it was that her doll arrived to me shorty after my book was released. Perhaps she found her way to me because she wanted me to know how much she appreciated me sharing her story.

ROBIN

It came as no surprise to me that, about the same time as Maci's arrival, I felt another urge to check out AJ's website to see if any more haunted items were up for adoption. With the amount of AJ items I have now, I always say Andrea and Tammy were influencing me to bring their old friends home to live with us. But, I digress.

On this particular evening in early 2013 while checking out AJ's website, I came across a photo of the largest blue eyes I'd yet to ever see on a doll. These eyes appeared wide with interest and seemed to be staring straight into my heart. It was a Chatty Baby doll manufactured around 1962. It remained in very good condition for its age and appeared hardly used. Upon reading the story of the doll, I can imagine why.

The original owner of the doll was a three year old girl named Robin who lived back in the early 60's when this doll came out. One sunny summer afternoon, her babysitter took her for a car ride to run some errands. The sitter, a college kid with no care for babysitting other than making money, decided to stop off at a bar for a drink. She left Robin in the car seat locked inside that car with the windows rolled up while she went into the bar for drinks. The sitter stayed in the bar for

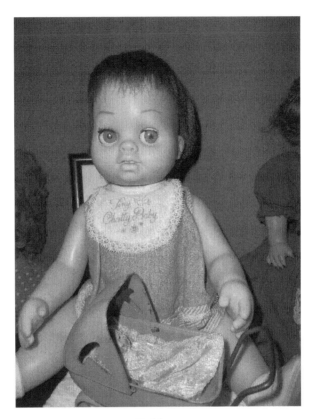

Robin

many hours, forgetting about Robin entirely. Unfortunately, Robin died in the car that afternoon from the heat exposure.

AJ reported that, while having the doll in her home, she captured many first class EVP's from Robin. It appeared the girl, much like the doll she haunted, was a regular chatty baby. Her little footsteps were often heard in otherwise empty rooms and AJ heard her disembodied giggles on many occasions. The doll's eyes often moved around on their own and never hesitated to follow visitors who entered the room.

When I received Robin, the second I pulled the doll out of the box, the doll's eyes met mine with fascination. I could feel her little spirit in there staring back at me. I smiled, welcomed her to my home and talked soothingly to her. I did notice even on that first day that the doll's eyes did seem to follow me as if watching me while I was going about my routines. However, I felt very comfortable with her there.

A few weeks later, I tried our first EVP session. Quite often, it takes a few tries with EVP to get a spirit to respond to me because they have to get used to me and gain trust. For Robin, this proved not the case. On that first EVP session, she automatically responded to me and even carried on a conversation with me from the spirit box which I could hear live as well as clearly on playback of the video recording I captured of the session. My first question was "Robin, are you here?" to which she automatically responded with "Yes....Kevin." I asked her if my other spirit children were treating her well, and she answered "Yes." Because she was a former AJ doll, I asked her if she remembered my girls Andrea and Tammy who also lived with AJ before. Robin answered "Yes." I made the comment about how sweet the girls are, and Robin once again said "Yes." I asked her for her age. She said "Three." Then, to my surprise, she called out my name.

"Kevin?" she called softly from the spirit box.

"What is it, sweet pea," I replied without hesitation.

"I love you," she said so sweetly to me.

I want to point out that it was the exact same little girl's voice who gave every response in this session. She did indeed sound like a very small child around the age of three. It was one of my most remarkable spirit box sessions I ever had with one of my haunted items. To this day, I play it back with fondness. When she tells me she loves me at the end, it never ceases to capture my heart.

A picture captured the image of Robin's spirit manifesting in the hallway.

During one of our sessions, Robin actually manifested herself to me in a photograph. After holding an EVP session, I began snapping photos around my great room. I thought I heard something moving in the main hallway that leads from the great room to the front door. I walked into the hallway. Sensing it might be Robin, playing in the hall, I asked her if I could take her picture. I told her how excited I would be for her to show herself to me for a picture. Though I didn't see anything with my naked eye, I snapped the next photo. Awesomely enough, a small apparition showed up in the photo. It appeared see-through and slightly faded. The figure appears to be that of a small girl wearing a white dress and gliding down the hallway past me. One can even see her hair trailing behind her if one looks at the photo close enough.

I have also had physical encounters that let me know Robin is about. For instance, around the spring of 2013 when Robin was still my only spirit of toddler age, I stood in the kitchen preparing myself some lunch on a Saturday afternoon. No one was in the house but me and my cat. As I stood at the counter preparing the food, I felt something solid brush against my leg just under the knee. It felt like a small figure rubbing against me. At first, I assumed it was my cat. However, when I looked down at my leg, the cat was nowhere to be seen. Quite surprised, I left the kitchen to look to see where the cat was. I found her curled up fast asleep on the window seal of my office which is across the house from the kitchen!

Something told my heart it had to have been Robin there in the kitchen with me, most likely brushing up next to me to watch me fix food. She is a very dear and loving child, and I enjoy every day of having her in my home.

CARLA

A young woman whose name I shall not mention contacted me regarding a very old doll she had in her possession. For the purposes of this story, I shall call her "Kelly." This young lady lived all the way up in New York City. She told me the doll belonged to her friend, but that her friend became so "creeped out" by the doll that she begged Kelly to take it into her home.

Not a believer in the supernatural, Kelly took the doll. It was a composition doll with its original wig still intact. Its legs however appeared to be in rough condition and she planned to get it to a doll hospital as soon as possible for much needed maintenance. Once the doll came into Kelly's home, it did not take long for her to realize what her friend was talking about when saying "creeped out."

Kelly placed the doll in a small wicker chair in her sitting area to be displayed. Just a few days later, she left for work. The doll sat in its normal place on the chair where she normally left it. That afternoon, she returned home. Going through the sitting area, she noticed the chair sitting empty. She looked around the room but found it nowhere. Kelly searched the house. When she reached her bedroom, she found the doll now sitting on her bed. Kelly froze, staring at the doll and wondering how it moved on its own. She lived alone and no one had been there who might have moved it.

The doll was placed back in its chair in the sitting room. A few days later, when Kelly returned home from work, once again the doll had moved. She searched the house. This time she found it in the guest room sitting near the window. This occurred several more times. Kelly would come home from work to find the doll missing from its chair. Each time the doll had relocated itself to a different place, and never the same place twice. The final time Kelly came home and had to search for it, she was shocked to find it lying in her clothes hamper at the bottom under a pile of clothes! It looked almost as though it were hiding from someone…or perhaps something.

Kelly also noticed the doll's eyes blinked on their own even when the doll was sitting very still in its chair. Sometimes, the arms of the doll moved on their own or the head turned by itself. Finally, after the

Carla's doll

incident with the clothes hamper, Kelly made her decision to finally rid herself of this doll. She decided to try to auction it off.

The doll sat for many weeks on Ebay up for auction before I was contacted, however Kelly received no bids. When I made an offer for the doll, Kelly jumped enthusiastically for the chance to rid herself of it. At that point, she was willing to take just shipping money alone to get rid of it. I covered her shipping cost, and she sent the doll to me where it came to live in its new home.

When I received this doll, I automatically felt a sadness from it. I felt no fear at all. The doll did not appear scary or malicious. It just looked very old, worn and tired. The doll had no clothing of its own, so I ordered the perfect little vintage doll dress for her. After welcoming her into my home and showing some attention to her, the spirit with this doll began to warm to me.

Just two nights after her arrival, I awoke to the sound of music coming from across the house. When I entered the kitchen from my bedroom, I realized the music came from the library room where I placed this doll earlier that evening. It sounded like flapper girl music from the 1920's. I started toward the library room, and the closer I got to the door of that room, the softer the music became. When I entered the door to the library, the music completely faded. Only the doll was left there sitting in her seat in the library. There are no radios, televisions or any other items in that room that might have caused the music to occur.

A few weeks after her arrival, I attempted EVP sessions. The second session was a success. I captured responses via the ghost box to a few of my questions. The voice was definitely that of a little girl. When I asked for her name, she responded "Carla." When I asked where she was from, she said excitedly, "New York!" I asked for her age, and she told me "Seven." However, I could not get a response from her as to how she died and what made her so sad.

Contacting my friend Doll Haven, I asked for her to do a reading with Carla's doll. Doll Haven sensed the little girl's spirit right off. She told me that Carla did die at a very young age. She lived a hard life and witnessed many scary events that took place around her. She would not talk about them and did not want to discuss how she died. Upon hearing this, I felt it best to leave that subject alone.

It seemed the reason the doll kept moving around on the prior owner Kelly was because of Carla's being afraid and feeling the need to hide. This would explain the doll's winding up at the bottom of a hamper hiding beneath a pile of clothes. What scared Carla? Why did she feel the need to hide? What horror(s) did she witness while alive? We most likely will never know.

While living in my house, Carla has definitely calmed down and seems very much at home with me. She no longer seems afraid. Her doll does not move away from its position where I have it sitting on a small table in my bedroom. I have however felt Carla's presence with her. Some visitors to my home have also reported seeing the doll move when they approached it to have a closer look. One such visitor, a member of a visiting paranormal team, sat in front of the doll and witnessed it raise its arm up toward her as if it were waving. Carla definitely does not mind having visitors or having her lovely old antique doll admired.

ELENA

Fellow paranormal investigators and haunted collectors often contact me to swap stories about items we've collected and various investigations we've been on, about the historical places we've visited and the encounters each place offered. On rare occasions, I might even receive contact from a haunted collector who actually wants to adopt out one of their items to me hoping to find a better home for it. Such was the case for my sweet little Elena.

An investigator, who I shall call Carmen for the purpose of this story, contacted me about an item she had in her possession for about a year that gave her some strange activity. Carmen's friend Genna purchased a house a few years ago in New Jersey. It was a two-story house with a spacious attic. On the day she moved in, Genna took some boxes up to her attic and found a doll lying up there. The doll was tall, twenty-seven inches in height, with long blonde hair, gigantic blue eyes, a porcelain head and limbs but a cloth body. Its outfit appeared to be something out of the early nineteen seventies. Everything about the doll appeared to be in mint condition though the doll had to be quite old judging by its clothing. Genna automatically called the prior owner and told her about the doll being left behind. The prior owner hurriedly assured her that the doll came with the house, to keep it at no extra cost and then ended the call.

Genna shrugged off the call and thought nothing more of it as she moved the rest of her things in. She left the doll sitting in the attic for the time being, standing it up against a stack of boxes, and began to settle into the new house. A week went by, then one evening Genna was in her bedroom preparing to go to bed when a thumping sound coming from the attic grabbed her attention. It sounded like small footsteps running back and forth across the attic floor. Her first thought was that some animal might have gotten into the attic. Being very cautious, she tip-toed quietly up the stairs to the attic, eased open the attic door and snapped on the light. Her eyes scanned the attic but found nothing. Nothing but the doll staring back at her from where she'd left it against the boxes.

For several nights after, Genna continued to hear the strange noises. The sounds escalated from small footsteps to what sounded like boxes and items crashing to the attic floor. Each time she inspected the attic, she found nothing out of place. Each time, the doll stared back at her from its position and gave her the chills.

Wondering if the doll had something to do with the noises, Genna decided to bring it down from the attic to a chair in her bedroom to see what might happen. Immediately after bringing the doll down, the noises in the attic ceased from then on. However, Genna did note that the doll always seemed to change positions by itself. Each time she came into her bedroom, the doll would be leaning in, or turned toward, a different direction than before. Believing the doll must be possessed by something, Genna decided to call on Carmen for help.

Carmen held an EVP session with the doll asking for information about whoever might be attached to the doll. On playing back the recording of the session, she discovered the voice of a small child captured. Her name was Elena. No other answers were given to Carmen's questions, but the little girl did leave a comment toward the end of the recording: "I want to play."

Elena

The idea of a haunted doll in her home proved to be too much for Genna, so Carmen took the doll into her own home. Once the doll entered Carmen's home, she also noted the doll changing positions by itself. Carmen felt at peace with having the little girl spirit in her home, however she felt the spirit wanted to find a forever home where she might have other spirit children to play with. When Carmen told me about little Elena, and I saw a picture of the doll with those gigantic blue eyes looking as if she were pleading to be loved, I simply could not resist. I immediately requested to adopt her.

The first day Elena arrived in my home, she became active immediately. After I took her doll out of the box and admired it, I placed it on the couch in the great room and left the room to go into the office to my computer to message Carmen that the doll arrived safely. While at my computer, I heard a sound coming from the great room behind me. It sounded like my cat Maddie's little yellow plastic ball bouncing across the hardwood floor. I thought perhaps it was just Maddie playing around, but still I went back into the great room to check it out. The cat was nowhere to be seen in the room. However, the yellow ball now sat on the floor next to the couch directly below where Elena's doll sat! I went off to look for Maddie and found her curled up asleep on the window seal of my bedroom across the house. A few minutes after, I did hear the ball bounce again on the floor but this time decided to leave little Elena to her play.

I waited a few weeks for Elena to settle in before trying my own EVP session with her. On the night of the session, I took her doll into the great room onto the couch. I set up my video camera to capture the session. Just after midnight, I started the recording, turned on the ghost box and began the session. I asked a series of questions and noted that I could definitely hear a little girl's voice responding from the ghost box although I could not make out what she said. After the session, I checked the video to make sure it did capture the session but decided to wait until morning to actually listen to the session.

The next morning, I took the video camera to download the footage from Elena's session to my computer. When I turned the video camera on, I found the video had mysteriously disappeared as if someone came behind me and deleted it. I have no explanation as to how this happened. The camera had definitely captured video, and no one else was in the house with me who might have deleted it.

Waving off defeat, I attempted the EVP session again the very next night. This time the video remained captured on my camera, and the voice response it captured was nothing short of a massive shock. When I played back the video the morning after and listened to it on my headphones, I heard the voices of two young males speaking from the spirit box. The statements were quite clear and were complete sentences, something that is normally unheard of from a spirit box. The box scans radio stations at a rapid speed of five stations per second, causing white noise and only a few short syllables to spill forth from those stations. A complete sentence from a radio station is definitely not possible on the spirit box. This was nothing short of supernatural.

What the male voices said also proved quite chilling. The first voice, clearly that of a teenage boy, shouted "You have to....you have to shoot me!" The second voice, in response to the first, was a deeper voice from another teen boy. It said, "Grab the purse!"

So, who were these young men speaking from my ghost box? And what connection did they have with Elena and her doll? Were these voices from spirits just passing through? Or did they have something to do with Elena and her death?

Drowning in my own questions and confusion, I decided to ask my friend, Doll Haven, for assistance. Without telling her what I'd heard on the recording, I asked her to take a look at the doll and let me know what she felt. Being a medium, she was able to pick up on Elena's spirit, and the visions she described brought chills.

Elena was indeed four years old when she died. On the night she died, she was spending the night at her Grandmother's house. Elena's older brother often ran with the wrong crowd. His friends were thieves and had a history of theft and altercations. The brother decided it might be a nice idea that evening to break into his grandmother's house and steal some of her antiques and jewelry to sell for money. His ring leader, a notorious thug, led the way to the grandmother's house. He told the brother to wait outside so his grandmother would not see him and recognize him. The ring leader proceeded to break into the house through a window.

Unbeknownst to them, the grandmother was still awake inside and heard the window open. Coming into the room, she saw the burglar and immediately screamed as high as her lungs allowed. In a quick effort to silence her, the leader pulled his gun and shot the grandmother in the chest, killing her immediately.

Little Elena was asleep in bed. The commotion awoke her and she entered the room to see the leader standing over her grandmother with the gun. She immediately began to scream in terror. The leader turn and shot Elena through the chest with no hesitation.

Outside, Elena's brother heard the shots. He raced to the window and climbed in to find his grandmother and his baby sister shot to death. He fell to his knees in remorse. Pleading up at his ring leader, he begged to be shot. The leader showed no sympathy whatsoever. Instead, he pointed toward the grandmother's purse lying on the floor nearby. "Grab the purse," he shouted.

Doll Haven's reading of Elena totally matched with the voices I heard from the EVP. When I told her of what I captured, we deduced that what I heard were voices from Elena's past hinting as to how she died. Elena had been terrified to see her grandmother shot to death by an intruder. She was so afraid when she saw the gun turned toward her. She never saw death coming. The voices from the ghost box showed me how terrible the scenario had been, the brother pleading to die with his grandmother and baby sister, and the gunman showing no emotion at all.

Since the session and reading, I made sure to give as much love and attention as possible to Elena. I assured her there was nothing more to fear and that her spirit was now free and well out of reach of evil. Since then, Elena has been quite peaceful. Her doll only moves slightly from time to time. Whenever I have it sitting next to me on the couch, it normally leans my way as if wanting me to hold it, and I do so with great love and affection. Elena has told Doll Haven that she is quite happy with me. Doll Haven asked Elena how she thought of me. Her adorable little response was, "He's nice."

THE DOLL CARRIAGE

Somewhere in Glendale, Arizona, sits an old house built around the 1890's. The house was filled with all kinds of strange items from dolls to paintings to crucifixes and other religious items. The current owners fled the property, leaving the house abandoned and alone. Where is this house exactly? What does it look like? As of today, this author possesses no answers to these questions. The family asked that their identity as well as the identity of the property remain anonymous at this time until they feel ready to share their story. For the past year, the Arizona Paranormal Search Team assisted this family and kept their identity anonymous. The family called on them for help when violent paranormal activity began to take place in the home. Some sort of unseen entity or entities attacked the family, even slapping and scratching some of the family members while inside the house. They fled and left their belongings, not wishing to ever return. When the team arrived to investigate, their encounters were nothing short of a nightmare.

On one of the nighttime investigations of the property, one of the team members entered a bedroom alone. The door slammed shut behind him followed by a disembodied evil cackle. The air turned to freezing so much that he saw his breath in front of his face. He rushed to the door and tried to open it, but the knob refused to budge. He screamed for help and banged on the door as loud as possible. Eventually, the door opened finally by itself and he fled. When he questioned his teammates as to why no one came to his aide, they responded that none of them even heard him screaming or banging. They never heard even a peep from the room while he was in there.

Scratching noises sounded on the wall. The family had quite a collection of antique items in their home. Many of the items began moving around on their own, disappearing from their places then showing up in an entirely new location in the house. In the room where the team member previously found himself locked in, the team checked the closet and found an antique doll carriage that appeared quite old. Judging by the design and condition, it was definitely made in the southwest and from the very-late 1800's. One of the team members announced that, hours earlier, he'd previously checked this closet and it was empty. Where did the carriage come from? The team leader contacted the owner of the property. However, the owner advised they knew nothing of any antique doll carriage in their home.

After many investigations of the home, the team deduced by the EVP's captured as well as the readings from their psychic medium that the house contained two groups of spirits, one quite good and one very much evil. The evil spirits apparently resided on the property for quite some time, most likely conjured up by some prior property owner in the past who dabbled in the occult. The good spirits, like angels of mercy, arrived to battle the evil spirits and protect the family. Unfortunately, this news proved not enough to change the current owner's decision not to return. He asked instead that the Arizona Paranormal Research Team aide in selling off the family's items in the home and bringing them the items they wanted to keep.

The team started posting auctions online for some of the items. In each auction, they did post a warning to all potential bidders that these items, though antique and quite lovely, came from a very haunted home and could most likely have a spirit attached to it. When I found out about the items, my curiosity refused not to be peeked. I checked out the items in their listings.

The mysterious doll carriage found in the closet stood out to me right away, so I contacted the team leader for more information. I learned that they did attempt EVP sessions around the carriage to test it. Nothing showed up in their EVP attempts. Their medium felt a very young, peaceful spirit was attached to the carriage but was quite shy and refused to talk. The item seemed safe to rehome, so I took them up on the offer.

When I received the carriage, I marveled at the great condition it appeared to be in and how fortunate I was to come into possession of such a possibly valuable antique piece. It seems the piece was made around the 1890's in the same time that the house in Glendale was built and might even possibly be an original piece to that house. Perhaps it was owned by one of the children of the original owner. Arizona Paranormal had no historical information to provide on the carriage, so I decided to try out some EVP sessions of my own with the carriage.

Using the spirit box and video, I conducted a late-night EVP session in the room where I kept the carriage. On the first try, I received

The doll carriage haunted by little Constance

several responses in the voice of a small girl coming from the spirit box. She told me that her name was Constance. She originally owned the carriage. She was five years old. She had a doll that went with the carriage, however she stated sadly, "I lost it." Heartbroken over this news, I immediately set out to find her a new baby doll to go with her carriage.

After a week, a found the perfect baby doll just the right size for the carriage and purchased it for Constance. I brought it home and placed the doll in the carriage with a small brown blanket that matched the color of the carriage. Later that night, I did another EVP session with the spirit box. Constance told me that she was very happy with the doll and decided to name it "Hannah." She also responded "Yes" when I asked her if she'd like me to take the carriage down from its shelf and place it on the floor for her to play with. So, I placed it on the floor for her.

Since then, I have made a point each night when going to bed to make sure to place Constance's carriage on the floor for her to play with. I keep the door to that room closed so the cat will not get inside unsupervised and tear anything up. I also keep a nightlight aglow in there just for my spirit children for their comfort. Sometimes in the mornings when I check on the room, I find the carriage has been slightly moved, and I know my little Constance has been enjoying her toy.

SANDRA

The haunted doll carriage was not the only item to come to me from the Arizona Paranormal Search team and the nightmare house they investigated. In my collection also sits a tiny doll not more than six inches high wearing a red velvet and gold dress. She was manufactured by Mattel back in 1967 as per the trademark on the back of her neck. The doll was among the many dozens collected by the owner of the nightmare home in Glendale.

The leader of Arizona Paranormal informed me that this particular doll was tested by one of her team members. Although no EVP's were captured, an odd occurrence took place upon completion of the session. The team member got ready to leave their headquarters for home and could not find his car keys! He looked high and low but the keys were nowhere to be found. Another member gave him a ride home. The next morning, when he returned to headquarters, the keys were found….lying right next to this doll!

When the doll arrived at my home, I immediately turned to friend Doll Haven for assistance. She did a reading of the doll and informed me

Sandra

that a little girl named Sandra actually haunted it. She is a playful spirit and loves to tease men in particular, hence the AZ team member losing his keys then finding them next to the doll a day later. Sandra spent most of her life ill in a sickbed. She had a particular illness that caused her to be paralyzed over most of her body and her speech to sound slurred. She lived to the tender age of eight then succumbed to the illness. She informed Doll Haven that she always wished in life that she could run and play with other children. Through Doll Haven, I told little Sandra to please feel free to run and play in my home….now her new home….as much as she pleases.

Since then, Sandra has proved to be a very sweet and loving spirit in my home. Sometimes I hear her playing, her little footsteps sounding on the wooden floor even in the daylight hours. I hear giggling coming from the room where her doll is located and I know it is her having a good time. She never plays tricks on me (none that I am aware of) but shows the upmost respect and a lot of love.

Sometimes, when I have Sandra's doll out with me, I feel a warm breeze brush by me, and I wonder if it's her letting me know she is there and having the time of her spirited life. What she did not have in this worldly life, she now enjoys in the afterlife. May she always run and play for the rest of eternity.

ALICE & ANNE

The day these young ladies arrived to me proved the most interesting that I've ever experienced to date in my haunted collecting. Their arrival was neither expected nor planned.

A friend of mine named Yazmin in Australia works in the paranormal field, specializing in demonology. She collected haunted items herself over the years which she kept in her home. However, when she started studying demonology and going into those types of investigations, she decided it best to adopt out her haunted items for fear she might bring home something bad one day that might have an effect on them.

When I perused the pictures of her collection, a beautiful 24 inch Alice in Wonderland doll haunted by a little girl named Amelia stuck out to me. Something about the doll's eyes called out to me to adopt her.

Yazmin granted my request. A day later, when preparing to ship the doll to me, she messaged me advising (quite slyly, I might add) that she was including a surprise inside the package with Amelia's dolls. She assured me the surprise would be a good one.

When the box arrived in the mail all the way from Australia, I took it into my kitchen and opened it. The curiosity over the "surprise" inside held fast to me as I cut open the box. Inside, Amelia's doll smiled up at me. Nestled on either side of her were two other dolls wrapped completely in packing paper. I took the mystery dolls out and unwrapped them. The sight of them almost made me scream.

Both dolls were painted over with the most grotesque looking design. One had black hair. Her porcelain face, arms and legs were painted grey and her eyes were completely painted black giving her an evil alien-like look. A small black X mark covered her mouth, while smaller X's rested on other parts of her face, all painted on with black paint. The other doll, a blonde, had the same grey paint over her face, arms and legs. Blood red paint covered her eyes and dripped down her cheeks.

Immediately, I felt nauseous. I placed the dolls down and got control of myself. Immediately, I wanted to message Yazmin and demand an explanation, but some strange feeling came over me that I had nothing to fear. These dolls were okay, not evil like their appearance suggested. I don't know where the feeling came from, but my nausea went away as quickly as it came. Looking back into the box, I found a handwritten note from Yazmin explaining who and what the dolls were. The dark haired doll was Anne, a four year old child who died from illness. Her older sister, ten year old Alice, haunted the blonde doll. She also had passed from illness. Both died a long time ago, possible in the 1800's.

Yazmin encouraged me not to be afraid and to please not let the appearance of the dolls fool me as there was an explanation. She

Anne and Alice

explained that she had the dolls for a long time. They never caused her a problem. In fact, the spirits were quite delightful. The dolls were once owned decades ago by an old woman in Shopshire, England, who dabbled in black magic. All of her neighbors feared her and steered clear of her house. She was quite mean and nasty to all who encountered her. At night, neighbors say they saw strange lights flashing from her house and assumed she was in the middle of her wicked spells. One night, her screams shattered the quiet atmosphere of the neighborhood. When the neighbors grouped together and went to her house to see about her, they found her lying dead upstairs next to some sort of weird drawing on her floor. The coroner ruled the death a heart attack, but those who knew her believe something evil must have come into her house and scared her to death.

The house was full of cats and all kinds of weird items that looked ritualistic. The dolls of Anne and Alice were found amongst the accumulated junk. Everything was sold off and the house closed up.

Anne and Alice have since passed from one owner to the next. Anyone who purchased the dolls never kept them for long. In recent years, they floated around on Ebay and other various internet auctions and dealer pages, however each time they were purchased, they never stayed with their new owner long and were posted right back on the internet for sale or auction. Each owner told of encountering the spirits of the girls with these dolls. The girls would cause electrical disturbance, and their disembodied voices and laughter were often heard near the dolls.

One prior owner did more research into the old witch who originally owned the dolls. He came across a more detailed account of these two particular dolls. The old witch painted them in such a grotesque manner because she wanted to use them as revenge dolls against her enemies. To this day, the names of those people are still written on the bodies of the dolls and hidden by their clothing. When she tried to use the dolls for vengeance, the precious little girl spirits refused to harm anyone. In a rage, she cursed them and caused them to be forever bound to the dolls.

Since Anne and Alice have been in my home, I have experienced those electrical disturbances and disembodies voices like the prior owners. However, I refuse to believe they are bound to these dolls. I believe they just choose to stay with them of their own accord possibly because the dolls looked like them or because they just plain like the dolls. Both spirits are quite peaceful and never cause a problem. My cat even seems to enjoy curling up near them sometimes.

On my first EVP session attempt with Alice and Anne's dolls, I managed to capture a full sentence from the spirit box from who I believe was Alice. At the time I held the session, my cat crept into the room, jumped on top of the nearby bookcase and knocked over some items sitting on top, sending them crashing to the floor. I marked the recording by saying "That noise was Maddie knocking some things over" so that when I played back the recording later, I'd know what the commotion was and that it was not something paranormal. When I played the recording back the next day, right after the point where I mention Maddie knocking things over, a little girl's laugh is heard from the spirit box followed by a complete sentence: "Look what you did, you cat!" There is a definite English accent in this child's voice, especially when she pronounces the word "cat". The voice is that of an older child around the age of ten, so I have no doubt that this is Alice's spirit commenting on my silly cat's antics. The voice does sound pleasant and like she found humor in Maddie's mishap.

Visitors to my home often cringe at first sight of Anne and Alice's dolls. I always tell them, don't let the physical appearance of these dolls fool you. Though the dolls themselves were painted hideously by an insane old woman, those two little spirits dwindling with them are not evil. They are very sweet little girls and nothing short of pure sunshine.

THE COBBLER'S STAND

A woman named Judy who resides in Missouri told me about an item she purchased at a yard sale near her hometown. She was browsing the curiosities and antiques when she came across an item that caught her attention. It dated back to the mid-1800's and its prestigious appearance instantly inspired her to buy it as the perfect antique item to display in her home. By all appearances, it seemed like an ordinary historical tool passed down through generations. The host of the yard sale assured her it belonged to an ancestor of his who once used it for his trade.

The tool in question is a cobbler's stand. It's simply a large block of wood with a cast iron anvil of approximately two feet in length protruding out from the top. Two cast iron shoe forms, one small and one large, came along with the tool. The shoe forms had square holes in them for them to be placed on the anvil for the cobbler to use to hammer shoe soles into place. In just gazing at it for a few moments, one can almost hear the clinging sounds of the cobbler hammering away at the shoe on the anvil.

Judy became instantly captivated with it. She placed the cobbler's stand next to her fireplace in the living room for visitors to see. The first few weeks, visitors who spotted the tool instantly took interest and questioned her about its origin. It quickly became a centerpiece for conversation.

One morning, Judy's seven year old daughter Tabitha came into the kitchen for breakfast. She told Judy of a dream she had about an old man in a vest and slacks who followed her around watching her every move. It spooked little Tabatha but otherwise posed no other concern. However, the next few nights, Tabitha continued to dream of the same old man following her around, never talking to her but rather keeping his distance and quietly observing her with interest.

The following week, Tabitha came into Judy's room in the middle of the night and awakened her. She told Judy that the old man from her dream now stood in her bedroom at the foot of her bed watching her. She refused to go back to her bedroom unless Judy came with her. Judy got out of bed and led Tabitha back to her bedroom. When they entered the room, they found it empty. Still, for the next few nights, Tabitha continued waking to find the old man standing there at the foot of her bed watching her with interest. She began sleeping in Judy's room and refused to go back to her own room after dark.

The haunted cobbler's stand

Judy remained baffled by Tabitha's experiences. They never had problems with her before. Never seeing the man herself on investigating Tabitha's room, she had no choice but to chalk it up to Tabitha dreaming and imagining things.

Less than a week later, Judy's teenage son Kenny came rushing into her bedroom after midnight shaking her awake. His friend was staying over that night and they'd stayed up downstairs in the living room watching movies after Judy and Tabitha went to bed. He now stood over her shaking her awake, calling to her with his eyes wide with fright. Judy sat up quickly.

"What's the matter," she asked.

"There's a man in the house," Kenny quickly said in a loud whisper. "He's downstairs. We saw him walking through the room."

Judy quickly got out of bed and followed Kenny out into the hallway. No sooner had they entered the hallway than they spotted an old man walking away from them in the shadows ahead. His backside faced them and he shuffled toward the stairs as if to return downstairs to the living room. He wore a black vest and slacks that appeared to be clothing from the 1800's. To their shock and surprise, instead of going down the stairs, the man stopped when he reached the end of the hallway, turned toward the wall.....and walked right through it, disappearing completely from their view.

Two and two clicked together quickly in Judy's mind. None of these issues happened until *after* the cobbler's stand entered their household. She decided that mere coincidence stood completely out of the question. The ghost had to somehow be related to that tool. The very next morning, she took the cobbler's stand out of the house and placed it into the garage outside. Once the stand left the house, the experiences ceased immediately. She never saw the old man again.

Knowing now that she held an authentic haunted item in her possession, Judy decided no other choice existed but to rid herself of the thing and its ghost. She posted the item online for sale, asking for a lower price than even she spent on it. Anything to rid herself of it fast.

I came across her online listing. Reading her description of the incidents she experienced in her home, and going by the fact this spirit never actually harmed anyone other than scaring the "bejeebers" out of them, I made the decision to take it off her hands. I contacted her, and she happily obliged me.

When the cobbler stand arrived, I placed it in my great room near my fireplace just like Judy had displayed it in her home. I called on my medium friend Doll Haven to have a look. As soon as she saw the stand, she immediately saw the old gentleman attached to it. His name is Bernard McFadden, she told me. When she described his story, it matched exactly with the story related to Judy by the cobbler's family who sold it to her. Bernard lived in Germany and worked as a cobbler in the 1800's. In the latter part of the 1800's, he immigrated to America to St. Louis, Missouri, where he continued his trade as a cobbler to the day he died from natural causes.

Doll Haven described Bernard as an older gentleman slightly stooped and wearing a black vest with slacks. His hands were gnarled from the years and years of work that he performed. He was a happy man but just slightly confused when his stand suddenly wound up in a strange home (Judy's home) away from his family. This is what triggered his nightly wanderings. He was curious about these strange people who now had ownership of his stand.

Since I spoke to Bernard and welcomed him into my home, asking him to make himself comfortable and feel free to be himself, Bernard no longer wanders restlessly. According to Doll Haven, he feels very content in my home. Though I've never seen Bernard's spirit, he often lets his presence be known to me. Sometimes very late at night when I am in my bathroom preparing for bed, or very early in the morning when I prepare to start the day, I hear the single, solitary clanking sound of metal on metal coming from the location of the cobbler's stand. The sound matches that of one of Bernard's shoe horns being placed onto the anvil or being tapped against it. Upon entering the great room to investigate the noise, of course I always find the stand and shoe forms untouched in their normal positions. But I know that the noise is Bernard letting me know he is there and that he is very happy to make my acquaintance.

THE MYSTERY PAINTING

A friend of mine whose name I shall call Mike approached me one day about a particular find of his in a recent visit to a garage sale near his neighborhood. Mike spent many years collecting paintings from garage sales, estate sales and antique sales. He enjoys collecting them for his home or to resale in his own business. The particular find he approached me with however caught him by surprise.

The painting, according to the prior owner, was done sometime in the 1940's and still sits in its original wooden frame. It is a portrait of an old woman possibly in her late sixties or early seventies. It captures her from her shoulders up. Dark shadows fill the background behind her, and a shadow also casts itself across a portion of her face. Though she faces forward, her eyes are cast off to the side as if looking at someone else. Her face holds an expression of anger or possibly even rebellion. The artist of the painting is unknown, and no artist signature can be found on the painting itself. Visitors to my home who see the painting often comment that the woman in the painting resembles a very angry Bea Arthur.

All kidding aside, Mike told me that he needed to get the painting out of his home as quickly as possible. His wife no longer wanted it inside the home or to be anywhere near it for that matter. The painting made her feel very uneasy even to the point of nausea. She could not explain why other than she felt there was something evil about it. Mike

The mystery painting

felt nothing odd from the painting and did not mind being around it. The ill feelings seemed only to be directed toward his wife.

I advised Mike that I would be happy to take it off his hands. So desperate was he to make his wife happy by removing it that he allowed me to take it for merely a few dollars though he paid more for it at the yard sale. I brought the painting home. I felt nothing odd from it, but the angry expression of the woman in the painting made me wonder. Just days after I hung the painting in the library room of my house, four different women who saw the painting came away telling me the painting gave them an ill feeling to the point of nausea. I wanted to know what the story was with the painting.

As has become my normal first order of business, I contacted Doll Haven. She gave the painting a reading and described the most interesting story to me. The artist of the painting was either the son or grandson of the painting's subject, and his spirit was the one who now haunted it. He studied art in school and desired to paint the lady's portrait for her. Her husband, a highly mentally abusive man, loathed art and refused to have his wife sit for a portrait. Tired of her husband's constant berating, the lady rebelled against him and sat for her portrait anyway. The young man painted the portrait under the stressful conditions. His final product proved a most excellent piece of art but definitely reflects the mood of the atmosphere in which he painted it. The woman's expression reflects her anger and rebellion against her husband. So upset was she that she refused to look directly at the artist while he was painting the portrait, hence the reason she seems to stare off to the side in the painting.

Doll Haven assured me that nothing evil resided within this painting. The negative residual energy from the circumstances when the painting was done lingered with it. This is what was causing the discomfort. Why this only occurred with women perplexes me, but I advised the spirit with the painting that I wanted him to behave and under no circumstances was he to make anyone in my home, living or dead, feel ill or discomfort. Since then, no one else has complained. Even female visitors come away feeling nothing but intrigue from the painting. The spirit seems to be behaving like a gentleman. I think he just wanted someone to take notice of his work and appreciate the hardship he went through to do it.

LAURA

When speaking of my friend Doll Haven, I cannot think of her without mentioning one of my most popular items in my collection. The item in question is a life-size doll of a little girl. So lifelike is her appearance that visitors who enter the library room of my house where the doll sits always mistake her for a real little girl sitting in my bean bag chair. She wears a silk dress with a dark suede top. Her long, curly black hair spills to her shoulders. Her dark eyes stare off with an expression of curiosity, and her skin with olive complexion appears smooth and flawless.

The little girl who haunts this doll is named Laura. She was twelve years old when she passed away, and her death is a tragic story that will tear out your heart. An assailant who to this day remains unknown kidnapped Laura. He took her off to an isolated place where he raped her over and over. In between raping her, he beat her violently. Eventually, the abuse became too much. Laura fell into unconsciousness and never woke up.

We don't know Laura's attraction to this lifelike doll that she haunts today. I suspect the doll possibly looked a lot like how she looked in life. Maybe she just likes the doll because she never got to have one like it before. In any event, Laura seems content with the doll.

I first saw Laura's doll in a photo posted by Doll Haven on her Facebook page. The doll belonged to Doll Haven and was one of her most prized possessions. The first time I saw it, I thought it was a real girl and possibly a picture of her daughter. Doll Haven reassured me it was indeed a doll, one made in France back in 1992. Something about the doll really grabbed my heart as I sat at my computer screen admiring the picture. I felt like her eyes stared back at me like she could see me

Laura

too. I felt very much drawn to her. I even felt like she was meant for me. I don't know where these feelings came from. Knowing the doll was not up for adoption, I quickly clicked away from the picture and went on with life.

It seems like only a month or so passed when one day I arrived home and turned on my computer to Facebook to find a major surprise. Doll Haven had a post with a picture on her page. The picture was of Laura's doll, and the post with it from Doll Haven stated "This really hurts me to do this. But Laura is up for adoption." It took me less than a second to pound out a message to Doll Haven requesting to adopt her. I certainly did not want to miss this opportunity. All the while, a chill passed over my body as I remembered my thoughts when I first saw the picture of Laura's doll, how I felt she was meant for me. Now, here she was available for adoption.

My ultra-speedy pounded-out message paid out as within minutes I became the happy new Spirit Dad for Laura!

Not long after Laura arrived, she wasted no time in making her presence known. I keep her doll sitting on my beanbag chair in the library room of my home where I feel she is most content. Each time I entered the room, I noticed her doll's head had turned on its own as if she were looking in a new direction every time I came in. Sometimes the sound of delightful laughter from a young girl came from the room where her doll stayed.

My cat Maddie remains fond of Laura. Sometimes I find her lying on the bean bag chair looking very content and snoozing away right next to the doll. When I have Laura's doll out on the sofa with me in the great room, Maddie is right there curled up next to the doll or even in its lap. One such evening while on the sofa with the doll and the cat, I turned to look at Laura to find her right hand lifted up by itself. The ring finger of the hand sort of points out as if pointing to something, so I automatically assumed she was pointing at something she wanted me to see. I looked around the room but saw nothing out of the ordinary. Looking back at the doll, I realized why she had her hand held up for me. Looking closer at the hand, I noticed the ring finger had small teeth marks in it where kitty tried to use it as a chew-toy. I recognize my cat Maddie's teeth marks anywhere now as she loves to chew things. I immediately scolded Maddie for her actions.

My first EVP session with Laura took place late one night in September of 2014. The first ten minutes of the session were a standard EVP session, and the last twenty minutes consisted of the use of the spirit box. I sat on the sofa with Laura's doll next to me as I carried out the session, the lights off and the room shrouded in darkness. As I asked a series of questions, I heard the sound of a car pulling up into the neighbor's driveway outside. A teenage boy resides there with the family, and apparently he returned home with a male friend of his that night. Through my great room window, I saw the two boys get out of the car. No one else was with them. Their voices sounded loud enough outside that I could hear them reverberating through my wall so I assumed they most likely just came from a party. They laughed and spoke out loudly as they walked from the car to the neighbor's front door. I made a comment out loud: "Oh great. Sounds like they're right outside the house." I said this as it upset me that the loud talking from outside might contaminate my recordings. This also served to mark the place where those voices would show up on the recording so I wouldn't mistake them for something paranormal when I listened to the playback later. I let the recording continue, but I waited on them to enter their house and for silence to take over once more outside before I continued my questions for the session.

The next morning when I played back the recording, I heard a voice right after my comment that excited me. A young girl's voice yelled "Stop" as if screaming at the boys. It sounded like a very young girl around the age of twelve or thirteen, the same age that Laura was when she died. The voice definitely came from close by me. I could almost picture Laura standing at the great room window yelling at those boys to "Stop" so I could continue my session. There were no girls outside. Only the two boys were seen and heard at the time of the session.

Three other responses showed up later in the recording when I played it back. During the spirit box session, I spoke to Laura about Maddie chewing on her doll's finger. I apologized about it once again. I said "She was a bad kitty, wasn't she?" Right behind this, a young girl's voice can be heard responding from the spirit box: "Ooooh....yeah!" I ask if Laura is there, and she responds "Yes." Several minutes later, I bounce the cat's ball across the room in order to get the cat to chase it, and from the spirit box can be heard a young girl's laughter as the cat is running off after the ball.

I gave Laura her own teddy bear as a gift, and she now holds it proudly in her lap as she still sits on the bean bag chair in the library looking toward the doorway and smiling as visitors come in. Whenever I do pick up her doll and hold her, I always feel a warm, strong positive injury there, and the doll's head never fails to come to rest on my shoulder automatically when I hold her close to me. Then, I remember back to the day I first saw her picture online, about how I felt strongly that she'd one day be mine, and I know... she is very happy to finally be home with me.

HEATHER

The most adorable encounter I've experienced before comes from my little singing angel Heather, another haunted doll adopted from my friend Doll Haven. The doll only measures about eight inches in height, but her soulful blue eyes which stare up at you with great curiosity possess the power to win anybody over. She wears a fluffy pink velvet dress with slippers, and her long dark brown curls spill down to her waist.

Heather was only four years old when she passed away. The specifics on her death remain unknown, but we do know she passed away because of injuries from a bad fall outside of her home. I call her my little singing angel because of her sweet, heavenly little voice I captured one evening from my spirit box.

During these EVP sessions with the spirit children, I like trying fun things to see if it yields a response from them. Sometimes, I try singing to them to see if they respond or maybe even sing back to me. In this session with Heather, I asked her if she knew the Alphabet Song. I then proceeded to sing just the first few letters for her: "A… B… C… D… E… F… G". At this point, I stopped and waited a few moments. To my

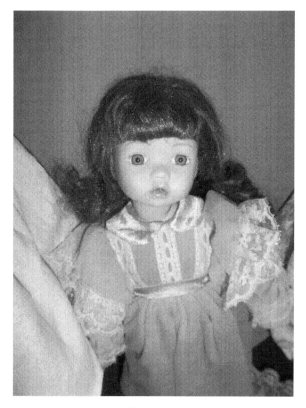

Heather

delight, the sweetest voice, that of a very small girl, sang back to me from the white noise of the spirit box: "A..B....C". She gave a short pause between the B and the C then drew the C out when she sang it, adding to the adorableness of her response. The voice sounded very soft and very high pitched like that of a four year old girl.

Another very pleasant little oddity that surrounds this doll is the scent of baby powder. Even on her first night in my home, when I stood Heather's doll on the sofa next to me, the aroma of baby powder wafted through the air around me. It lingered for a few seconds then vanished as suddenly as it came. The aroma has occurred several times around her doll no matter what room I might have her in. I believe the scent comes from Heather's spirit as a signal that her precious spirit is near.

Heather brings nothing but delight to my home, and every time I hold her doll, I feel an extremely pleasant energy radiate from it. Perhaps one night she might entertain me with another song and let her sweet voice sing to me once again from the spirit box.

THE ISLAND BABY

Probably the most popular item in my collection just arrived to me recently in January of 2015. This item is an antique composition doll at least one hundred years old. Its head and hands are made of a hard plaster but the rest of its body consists of cotton and cloth. His name is Harold. My first remark should be that this doll should not be confused with the famous Harold The Doll owned by Anthony Quinata. No, mine is totally different, but they do share a common denominator.

Most people who watch the show *Ghost Adventures* on the Travel Channel or are just plain hardcore ghost fans have heard of the Island of the Dolls located in Mexico. The island rests in the canals off the coast of Mexico City and to this day remains completely inhabited by dolls of all sorts. Some hang from the trees while other rest in the "doll museum", a shack of sorts which sits in a central part of the island. The original caretaker of the island, Don Julian, began the doll collection on the island around fifty years ago order to appease the spirit of a girl who drowned just off the banks of the island. Don Julian actually found the body of the girl floating in the water and became haunted by her death. Shortly after, the spirit's cries of misery and loneliness were often heard coming from the island. Don Julian began bringing dolls to the island for the tiny spirit to play with. This helped to bring peace to the girl, and her cries subsided. Since then, to this day, locals and the curiosity seekers still flock to the island to check out the macabre display of dolls and even donate their own for the collection. Many believe that almost each and every doll on that island holds a spirit that haunts it.

Interest in the Island of the Dolls recently renewed when *Ghost Adventures* aired in an episode about an investigation they held on the island. So intent were they to get a reaction from the haunted dolls there that they brought along Anthony Quinata's famous Harold The Doll, a very haunted doll said to be possessed by a very dark entity, to see how he and the island dolls would react to each other. Some evidence, including a child's laughter heard on an EVP recording, was captured during the investigation.

My Baby Harold doll was among those donated to the island and once resided there. He has since left the island prior to the *Ghost Adventures* filming when a relative of Don Julian removed several of the older dolls to make room on the island for more to be brought in. Otherwise, it would have been interesting to see how Baby Harold and the bad Harold would have reacted to each other. Unlike Harold The Doll, my Baby Harold holds a spirit who is quite gentle.

The doll Baby Harold haunts once belonged to his family and carries a tragic story attached with it. The real Baby Harold lived to only nine months old. He lived with his mother in an apartment building. His mother collected dolls, and this particular doll belonged to her collection. One night after Harold and his mom were fast asleep, a fire started in their apartment. His mother had drank heavily earlier that evening and still remained in a stupor. She awoke to the flames. In her state of drunkenness and being half asleep, she grabbed for Harold and stumbled out of the apartment. Unfortunately, when she got outside, she realized she had grabbed one of her dolls by mistake.

Fighting her way back through the flames, the mother re-entered the apartment in a desperate attempt to save her baby. Unfortunately, she never made it back out. Both Harold and his mother died in the fire that evening. This particular doll of mine was one of the items which made it out of the fire. Whether it is the doll Harold's mother grabbed in error is unknown. But, to this day, the smell of smoke still lingers around the doll.

The family of Harold's mother kept the doll for many years before bringing it to donate to the island. They reported many strange incidents around the doll. It moved on its own on many occasions. Harold's cries and even laughter were heard coming from it on some occasions. They believed the poor baby's spirit now haunted the doll and began calling the doll by his name.

Baby Harold remained on the Island of the Dolls within the doll museum for a few decades. Several years ago, after Don Julian's passing, one of Don's relatives removed some of the dolls from the island in order to make room on the island in case of further donations from curiosity seekers. Harold was one of the dolls removed. The

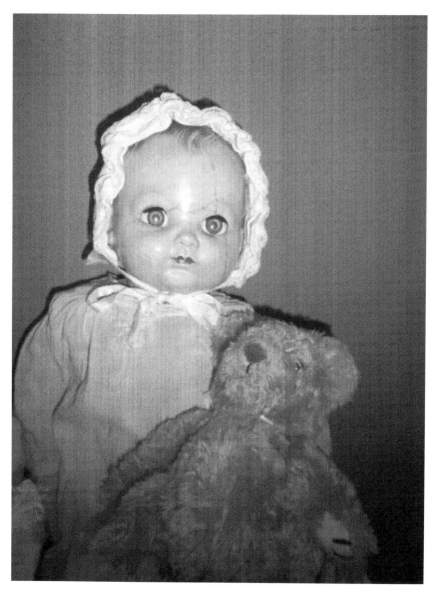

Baby Harold, the island doll

relative kept the dolls in his own home until his wife grew too afraid of them and asked that he rehome them.

I came into contact with the last owner of Baby Harold when she needed to rehome him after a bad occurrence (not related to Baby Harold) occurred in her home. She began experiencing attacks from a demonic entity in her home and decided to rehome the haunted items in her possession. When Baby Harold came up for adoption, I held no intention of passing him up.

When Baby Harold arrived, I took him out of the box. Immediately, his eyes blinked. I held him up in my arms like a child and looked into those eyes. It felt like something peaceful was staring back at me. The eyes blinked again. The head then lolled to the side on its own and came to rest lovingly on my shoulder. Harold was now in his forever home. I think he's happy.

Since Harold's arrival, I have not heard any crying from him as has been reported in the past. His eyes blink on occasion and he changes position sometimes. I've experienced nothing at all alarming from this doll. The smell of smoke does waft past me on occasion when I stand or sit right next to his doll reminding me of his presence there. I believe though the he feels peace in his surroundings and loves his new spirit daddy. I welcome him to my home and hope he experiences nothing but peace going forward.

OTHER ACTIVITIES

A lot of activity occurs within my house, and with so many spirits now lingering here, one might never know which spirit might be causing what activity whenever something happens. On many occasions, I have felt a little hand tug on my shirt or come to rest on my arm or hand, and in those cases I know it is one of my spirit children letting me know he or she is there. I might not know which one but I always give a smile and tell them how wonderful it is to have them here.

Probably my favorite activity occurred one night when I went to bed. I crawled under the covers and relaxed. The cat jumped onto the bed and curled up next to me purring away. I lay there stroking her and listening to her purr. Only a few seconds passed when suddenly I felt another form, that of a small child, lie down next to me on the other side of the bed from where the cat curled up. I lay there waiting, and before long, another form lay down toward the foot of the bed next to my legs. On the other side from there, another little form lay down near the foot of the bed. I simply smiled, said goodnight to them and told them how much I loved them. On several occasions I have felt this happen. Sometimes it might be one spirit child and sometimes two or three might lie down with me.

My spirit children, just like normal children, get curious and love to go around my house checking things out. On a few occasions, I've sat on my sofa in the great room watching television and heard my bedroom closet door open and shut by itself during the evening hours when no living soul is in there. Upon checking it out, I always find the door shut as if nothing happened. The cabinet doors in the kitchen are also often heard opening and closing on their own normally when I am not in that room. Much like the bedroom closet, I always find the cabinet doors closed and everything looking normal when I try to check it out. The noise always stops before I enter the room.

When I have guests in my home, I always ask that they not touch the dolls. I do this because I never know how the spirit of an item might react to someone touching his/her item. Some spirits don't like their items to be touched very often. Most of my spirit children love for me to pick up, hold and carry around their dolls that they haunt. I've never had an issue of my own. However, my young nephew once had a shocking experience when he started to pick up one of the dolls. The doll in question is Patty's doll.

The incident occurred on my first night moving into my new house. On this particular evening my sister and her family were visiting my new home to help me unpack. My nephew, who was seven years old and rambunctious at the time, went into my bedroom and spied Patty's doll lying on the bed where I left her. I and my sister happened to be in the room at the time getting things into place. My nephew went over and started to grab up the doll to check her out. As soon as his hands came to rest on the doll and began to lift her, he suddenly dropped her from his grasp and grabbed his arm, an expression of pain flashing across his face.

"Something pinch me," he said. He immediately hurried from the room.

A few hours later as my sister and I unpacked items in the great room, we heard my nephew's voice coming from my bedroom. Apparently, he'd mustered up enough courage to return to that room regardless of his earlier pinch from Patty. Though he was the only one in that room at the time, we heard an additional voice, one barely audible, talking with him. We walked toward the bedroom door, and the second voice stopped talking. We heard my nephew clearly saying one word over and over and laughing while doing so: "Boo! Boo! Boo!"

When my sister attempted to ask him who he was talking to, he refused to answer. He only grinned as if being coy and secretive. One thing that surprised me about this is that Patty's doll has its own toy which I purchased a few months earlier for Patty to play with and, if I may be so honest, to be used as a trigger object. The toy in question is a tiny stuffed monkey doll which Patty's doll holds in her arms at all times. I lovingly named the monkey doll for her when I purchased it. The monkey's name is Boo.

Had Patty spoken to my nephew, making friends with him at last and actually telling him the name of her favorite stuffed monkey toy? To this day, he does not say. The secret I guess remains held between him and Patty.

Though Patty seemed to make friends with my nephew after, the fact that she pinched him for attempting to grab her doll (most likely with the intentions to rough-house with it), I always tell everyone to please not touch my haunted items when visiting my home. I do this not only for their safety but also out of respect for those sweet spirits who make their home with me.

An obvious activity experienced often in my house is the sound of disembodied voices talking. On some occasions I hear the voices of a child or children coming from one of the rooms where the dolls and items are located. The most talkative are the spirits of teenage girls who haunt a few of the dolls located in my library room. I hear their voices chattering away, even giggling, but the moment I enter the room, the chattering ceases. Spectral smells are also common. Most of the time the aroma is that of flowers or that of baby power, although I have neither of these in or around my home. I believe the flower smells might be from the teenage girls and adult female spirits as the smells always seem to come from near those items they haunt. The smell of the baby powder always lingers around the dolls with the child spirits, like Heather. Luckily, I have experienced no smells from the male spirits.

My spirits have acted as my wake-up call on a few occasions. One morning on a work day, my alarm went off waking me from deep sleep. I reached out and slapped the button on the alarm clock to quiet it then dosed back to sleep. This particular morning happened to be on a work day, so dosing back off certainly put the wheels in motion for me to be late getting out on time and getting to work. Fortunately, one of the spirit children decided to wake me. I felt the mattress move up and down right next to me. It felt as if a child were there right next to the bed pressing her hands down onto the mattress to cause it to go up and down. The sensation was gentle but enough to capture my attention. I opened my eyes but saw no one there.

A similar instance occurred on a work morning where my alarm woke me but I slapped the button to shut it off. I dozed back off for a few minutes then came right back awake when the sound of a fist knocking sharply on my closed bedroom door caused me to sit straight up in the bed. It was high on the door and sounded like someone were standing on the other side knocking to rouse me up and answer the door. Getting out of bed and going to the door, I opened it to find no one out there. I do have a few items haunted by adult male spirits. Perhaps one of them was assisting in getting me up and moving for the morning.

There have been times when I've heard a loud crash come from one of the rooms where my haunted items are kept in my house. The sound is always like a bookshelf falling over, or perhaps some of the dolls falling from their shelves to the floor. Of course, when I go to investigate, no source of the noise can be found. All of the items always appear to be in place.

Lights always seem to provide a source of entertainment for ghosts. The lamp in the great room of my house seems to go crazy sometimes when I bring one or two of the dolls out. The lamp sits right next to the sofa where I normally sit to watch television at night. On quite a few occasions, I've noticed the lamp blink off and on as if someone were playing with it. Every time this happened, I had one of the dolls sitting with me on the sofa. Most likely, the blinking of the light was the spirit's way of letting me know that he/she was there.

Probably my most favorite supernatural occurrence with my haunted items involved my cat and the fireplace. A gas fireplace sits in my house in the great room. Inside the fireplace, small black rocks cover the bottom beneath the gas logs as a sort of decoration. My cat Maddie, being curious as most are, loved to reach her paw between the screen and the fireplace opening and scoop out the rocks. I scolded her on many occasions for fear she might get hurt or burned getting that close to the fireplace. One cold night in the late fall of 2013, I spotted Maddie slinking toward the fireplace. At the time, the fire was on in the fireplace. I was sitting on the sofa, and I stood up immediately to yell for her to stop.

Before any words came from my mouth, the cat suddenly rose up, her paws completely leaving the floor as if someone gently picked her up. Still in the air about an inch or so off the floor, Maddie went backwards as if someone were pulling her away from the fireplace. Her paws went straight out and she turned her head from side to side as if in shock at being picked up. She was carried backwards about five feet before whoever carried her let her drop softly back to the floor. She immediately fled the room.

Knowing right away that whoever it was (most likely one of my spirit children) pulled Maddie was doing so out of care, I thanked the spirit aloud for helping to protect my kitty cat. Since then, Maddie is always friendly to each of my items. Whenever one of the dolls is brought out to the sofa in the great room, she curls right up next to the doll and rests her head lovingly on the doll's lap. She sleeps quite heavily and peacefully with them, a good sign to me that only positive spirits reside with these dolls and items.

The spirit children love to play with Maddie. Many times I've sat and watched her racing around the room or through the house as if chasing, or being chased playfully by, something only she can see. Sometimes she walks into a room and her tail goes straight up, the tip end forming over into a curl, a reaction she normally has when someone familiar to, and loved by, her enters a room. She curls her tail up for me in the same manner whenever I return home from work. When I am alone in the house and I see her walking away into another room, her tail curled up in that same manner, I know she is seeing one of those positive spirits she and I love so dearly. Never has my cat shown any fear or negative reactions toward these spirits and the items they haunt.

PART FOUR:

Some Questions You Probably Have

So, I thought I would dedicate this part to the questions I get asked the most every day when I speak about my haunted collection, do panels at conventions or festivals about it or get interviewed about it. Haunted collecting is a subject indeed that spurns many questions. No doubt someone shall read this book and find their interest in collecting haunted items peeked. With that said, along with the answers to the top questions I'm presented with, I also shall include a warning....yes, a warning.... about getting into haunted collecting or any other portion of the paranormal field for that matter.

Haunted collecting is no matter to be taken lightly. It is not meant for thrill-seekers looking for adventure. It is not meant for anyone who has not had at least some training or teaching in the field of paranormal investigating. Just because you watch or have watched every episode of *Ghost Hunters* or *Haunted Collector* or *Ghost Adventures* does not an expert make you! In fact, I shall go to the point (at the risk of insulting some of those involved in the media) that possibly not all of what you see and hear on television or in the movies is real. The only true guaranteed knowledge you can obtain is by studying and participating in investigations yourself.

Are you interested in ghost hunting? Want to become a member of a paranormal investigation team? I believe almost, if not every, state in this country has at least one or two paranormal teams handling that state in order to assist those with possible paranormal issues in their home, business, school or etc. Do a search of the internet for paranormal teams in your area. You may be surprised how many real teams you may find. Once you do find one, pick one who is the most legitimate, and contact them to see if they are looking for new members.

Another idea for a search would be for paranormal classes. Some teams offer courses in paranormal investigating, even Paranormal 101 type classes, that help you better understand the seriousness of investigating hauntings and other paranormal occurrences. This partnered with actually joining in on paranormal investigations as a "rookie" investigator can help educate you better and more properly on the subject.

Investigating the paranormal is no joke. This is something quite real and not meant to be played with or messed with by those who do not know what they are doing. Not all spirits are good. Bad spirits, including demonic entities, do exist in our world and can attack when least expected. Only those who are highly trained and qualified should be called on to handle such issues.

With this being said, I shall now present the top questions and answers I'm normally presented with in my odd yet interesting past-time.

Why are items haunted?

Paranormal investigators and experts will each have a different opinion on the answer to this question. Some believe items become haunted because of the item being used in a ritual or witchcraft to summon an entity or demon. Others believe the items are cursed. For everyday people with no experience in the paranormal world, most believe automatically that if something is haunted, it must be by a demon. This belief is most likely caused by so many movies and shows about killer dolls and demon-possessed items. Not many of these shows would portray an item haunted by a good spirit as that would defeat the purpose of being scary.

My personal belief is that a spirit haunts an item just simply because it chooses to do so. No magical mumbo-jumbo. It's just a free choice. A spirit might choose to haunt a doll or an item because he/she once owned that item and treasured it. In the case of a haunted doll, a spirit might also choose to linger with it because it reminds him/her of a relative, a lost love or even him/herself. Whatever the reason the spirit chooses, I believe the spirit resides with the item completely by free choice.

Being free spirits no longer imprisoned within physical bodies, they pretty much come and go as they please. It has been my experience that spirits who haunt items don't always stay inside or with that item 24/7. In my home, the spirits who haunt my collections tend to roam the house of their own free will. They open doors, knock on walls, play with the cat then return to their items whenever they feel like it. They tend to always return to their items as those items they choose act as an anchor for them. Wherever that item goes, the spirit will haunt that location the item is housed in. But they can still roam as they want to.

Sometimes all will be quiet in my house for two or three weeks, and I know the spirits of my collection are either at peace or temporarily roaming elsewhere. Then, after a few weeks of silence, activity begins to build again and may last off-and-on for days. So far, I have been blessed in not ever having anything negative happen in my home but I have been very careful in choosing what items I bring in.

Can anyone be a haunted collector?

At the risk of disappointing, I must say that haunted collecting isn't for everyone. Not just anybody can take in haunted items and know how to handle them or deal with them. It does take experience with the paranormal and paranormal investigations. If you have a serious interest in the world of ghosts, I always say you should school yourself first before trying to go head-first into paranormal investigations. There are some…in fact many….evil and demonic entities out there that like to fool people and cause harm, even physical harm such as scratching, biting and even burning their victims. For your own protection, make sure you educate yourself first and find out if the paranormal field is the right one for you.

No doubt people will watch television shows and/or movies about hauntings and paranormal investigations and get the desire to go out and seek a thrill, trying to be like those people they see in the shows. For the sake of your own safety and the safety of others, please leave paranormal investigations to the professionals.

I am experienced and have decided to collect haunted items. What do I look (or look out) for in collecting haunted items?

Just couldn't resist it, could you? Well, if you are interested in starting your own home museum of haunted artifacts, first thing you need to know is this: you are doing so at your own risk. Please take caution when looking to obtain haunted items and know what you might be getting yourself into.

The best thing to look for in your haunted item search is an experienced collector or investigator who may have items that need to be "rehomed" (meaning the items need to go to a new home). Sometimes collectors need to make space for other items so they decide to rehome certain items they feel are safe and ready to be placed up for purchase or adoption by someone serious in wanting to obtain such items. There are many avenues online where you can search out collectors rehoming their items. Facebook for instance has several groups of serious collectors who have experience with items.

Creepy Dolls & Paranormal Experience, a group founded by avid doll collector and paranormal investigator Sherrie Schoon of Georgia, includes many people with experience with such items and who often seek to rehome items when they are ready. Sherrie herself sometimes makes haunted dolls from her own collection available for adoption on the group's page to serious collectors with experience.

Anjie Calvin Miller, the founder and owner of AJ's Haunted Dolls and who is also a medium and paranormal investigator, also provides opportunities to adopt haunted dolls which she has collected and might need to rehome. The spirits of her dolls range in age from infant and toddler on up to adult. All of her dolls are kept and tested by her normally at least two or three years so that she may gain knowledge of who or what is attached to the item before placing it up for adoption. This way, interested collectors can know ahead of time what they are adopting, and AJ can determine whether the spirit is positive and okay for adoption or whether it might be something negative that must be dealt with properly. It also gives the adopter a chance to know the spirit's story before adopting the item. Several of my dolls were adopted from her and have proven to be a delight to have in my home.

Doll Haven, a business run by medium Sherri Richardson, also provides amazing opportunities to adopt dolls with delightful spirits of all different age ranges. Many of my dolls come from her, and each has given me wonderful activity. Sherri also takes the time to get to know and understand the spirit, whether it is positive or negative and whether or not it is safe to adopt out before making the item available for adoption.

What you definitely must look out for are dealers who are placing items on auction sites and online stores falsely claiming they are haunted just to make a major buck. In my search for paranormal items, I came across some of the most bizarre listings that I knew right away had to be a hoax to make money. One auction for instance listed an item haunted by a famous celebrity (who shall remain unnamed) and listed the starting bid price for four thousand dollars. Was this item really haunted by said celebrity? Most likely not. I would venture to guess some fraudulent seller only wanted to make money from an unsuspecting paranormal fan with no experience in haunted collecting.

Another serious issue might be that the item is indeed haunted but by an inhuman demonic spirit that might cause harm. The seller might post the item falsely as being haunted by a nice spirit in order to get rid of it quickly. This is not the way to go about getting rid of an item haunted by a negative spirit (more on that later) and any seller being fraudulent should be reported to the auction site.

Some sellers turn out to be legitimate. Some paranormal teams put up haunted items that they rescue from abandoned homes up for auction once the item has gone through proper testing. The only way to find out who is legitimate is to check them out. Look at their feedback as a seller. Is it negative? Even if there are only a handful of negative remarks in the feedback, check those comments out to see what the complaint regarded. Ask questions of the seller. Probe them to find out where the item came from and what evidence they have to back up the item being haunted. Also, don't be afraid to ask questions to fellow paranormal enthusiasts on respectable paranormal pages about any seller you have questions about. You may be surprised what you can find out from people who might actually know said seller and can vouch for or against that seller. It always helps to do what you can to protect yourself from scammers.

Once you have adopted a spirited item into your home, remember that it is not a toy and not meant to be played with. Respect it and keep it clean and in a safe place. Too many times people adopt items expecting a show. For instance, one might adopt a haunted doll hoping to see the doll itself get up, walk around and talk like something from a horror film. Please do not adopt an item just because you want to see a show. Most haunted dolls do not get up and walk around, at least not the ones haunted by human spirits. These spirits are more or less *with* the doll, not *inside* the doll. Though they might cause the doll to turn its head or move it arms and legs once in a while, do not expect them to make the doll get up and dance.

Think of it this way….you are adopting the spirit of a person into your home. Treat them respectfully as you want to be treated. Make them feel at home. I always tell my new arrivals to make themselves at home, that my home is their home and to just feel free to be themselves. Talk to them often and show them attention. They love to feel wanted and to get attention, especially the spirit children. Do not just leave their item on a shelf to collect dust with no attention whatsoever as most likely you shall get no activity from the spirit. Show them attention, and they will give you the same.

What if a bad spirit comes into my home?

People often make the mistake of attempting to destroy items when they find a negative spirit or demonic entity attached to it. They burn the item, bury it, throw it in the garbage and etc. This does nothing to rid yourself of the spirit. If you destroy the item, you are not destroying the spirit or entity. You are only destroying its vessel, which will most likely anger it and make things worse.

The best thing to do is look for the proper assistance in removing the item from your home. Are you a member of a church? If so, contact your pastor/minister/priest for assistance or advice. Let the church help you if they can. If you do not have a church family, check your local listings or even the internet for a demonologist or paranormal team closest to your area. They can most likely come to safely take away the item for you. You can also find help online in groups such as "Creepy Dolls and Paranormal Experience," a group hosted by Sherrie Schoon (mentioned earlier in this section) on Facebook. They can offer assistance or advice on how to properly rid your home of the haunted item and perhaps even offer to take it off your hands.

Bottom line is this: do not try to get rid of the item on your own. Seek out the proper professional help to keep yourself, your home and your family safe and secure.

Do You Do Anything To Protect Yourself?

Here is where I want to turn this into a ministry opportunity. My first and foremost means of protection….is my savior Jesus Christ. He is the ONLY protection I need against evil spirits. When I was eleven years old, I gave my life to Christ and to date have not been disappointed. I have never been in need for anything. I have always had plenty of food, a wonderful home, family and friends, and many wonderful blessings in my life because I trust in Him for protection and forgiveness of my sins.

Every night I say a prayer over my home asking God in Heaven, in the name of Jesus, for protection over my home, to cast away Satan and his demons and keep out all evil and intruders. So far, this protection works splendidly. I've never had a bad encounter in my home and never had any problem from an angry spirit or evil entity. My home remains totally serine and my wonderful spirit family stays happy and content in the home with me. Even my cat loves being around all of my items and stays happy, healthy and full of life. If you do not have faith in the Lord, I strongly recommend you re-think your situation as faith in God is the strongest protection you can ask for.

As the sort-of gravy-on-top, I do have several rose quartz crystals scattered within my home. These crystals are believed by science to give off an aura that makes one feel more relaxed and positive. Paranormal experts believe they also keep positive spirits happy and keep away negative or evil spirits. Is this true? It just might be. Can I do without them? Absolutely because of my faith in Christ! However, it's nice to have that extra little boost of positive energy in my home given off by such a beautiful mineral created by God himself.

So, Why Do Spirits Even Haunt Items? Why Don't They Just Go On To Heaven?

I've heard several different answers given to this question from many colleagues in the paranormal field. Some say when the person dies, the spirit sort of waits here for a guide to come and lead them to the other side. Another explanation is that there is no heaven or hell and that we just wander free as spirits once we die.

I do believe in heaven and hell. I do believe in God. I also believe that human spirits can indeed wander free amongst us, but I believe there is a more amazing reason as to why they wander here.

In the Bible in the book of I Thessalonians, Chapter 4, starting with verse 16, it states "For the Lord himself will come down from heaven with a loud command, with the voice of the archangel, and with the trumpet call of God, and the dead in Christ will rise first. After that, we who are still alive and are left will be caught up together with them in the clouds to meet with the Lord in the air."

The Christian faith believes the Lord Christ who died on the cross then rose again on Easter morn ascended to heaven and will come again to take all of us who have faith in him to be with him in heaven. Meanwhile, those who pass on before that time are sort of in a waiting period. Is it limbo? Purgatory? I like to believe it is a safe realm, sort of a "waiting room", if you will, where spirits go away from harm, away from evil and away from pain and simply wait on Christ to return.

Those entities who remain roaming the earth, possessing people, causing havoc, throwing dishes around in haunted houses and scratching innocent people are most likely the souls of evil people or just plain demonic entities. The gentle spirits however who quietly make their presences known, who gently caress us and watch over us, are those souls who chose the right path and, along with the angels, seem to watch over us as they wait for the end of time to come.

Not everyone will believe this theory. Not everyone shares the Christian faith. I do believe however that this is how the spirit realm works. Those spirits who are saved in God shall rise to heaven when the time comes, while the spirits of those who committed evil or just plain chose the wrong path to follow, must remain behind. It all hinges on what choice you make in life while you still breathe. Do you choose to follow God? Or do you choose to follow the world which the devil enjoys roaming and misleading the innocence? Our very fates do hinge on that ultimate life decision.

A Final Word of Warning

Though I have probably stressed it a dozen times in this book, I cannot stress enough how dangerous the investigation of the paranormal can be and feel compelled to repeat it again before bringing this book to a close. It alarms me how many "thrill-seekers" out there tune in to ghost hunting shows on television then want to go out with their friends on Friday or Saturday night, find a haunted place and try to be like those guys on television. Please, if you are one of these people, do yourself a favor and leave the investigating to the professionals.

There are in this world evil spirits who harbor themselves among us. They do not hesitate to attack the unknowing innocents when least expected. They want our souls and will stop at nothing to gain them. They can do so by physical attack or just by simply blinding us with stupidity. If you go seeking trouble, most likely you will find it, or it will find you. So, for your own safety, please have respect for the world of paranormal investigating and leave it to those with experience.

Many people come under attack by evil forces in their own homes, in their places of business and even out in the open. These people come to paranormal investigators seeking help and guidance. Anyone who does not take such investigations seriously may cause more harm to their clients and even harm themselves. No one should go into joining or creating a paranormal team just for the fun of it or just to see a ghost. It is a serious business meant to help those in need of spiritual aide. For one to want to become a paranormal investigator, he/she must not only possess a strong interest to investigate the unknown but should also be aware and leery of the consequences of dealing with the unknown and must, above all, possess the passion to help others understand what they are dealing with and how to live with or combat it. For an average every day person, encountering a ghost can be quite frightening, especially in said person's own house. Don't you think said person deserves an experienced, caring, understanding ear when the call for help?

The world of the unknown is quite fascinating, and let's face it, who doesn't love a good ghost story? But please understand that along with ghosts and other fascinating elements hovering unseen around us in the world of the unknown, there also lurks evil and danger around almost every corner. The business of the paranormal is definitely not for the untrained or the weak at heart.

About The Author

Kevin Cain grew up in the south reading, listening to and enjoying the wonderful storytelling of times gone by. His favorites were always ghost stories, and they inspired and enthralled him to write his own. Kevin has published short stories and novels about the paranormal, including his recent novel *Patty Doll* about a haunted doll that resides in his own home. Kevin resides in central Alabama where he lives with his cat and the wonderful, peaceful spirits who enjoy making their home with him.